Disclaimer:

The contents of this book are memories and events from the Author's past. Some names and identifying details of people or places described in this book have been altered to protect their privacy.

This book is dedicated to everyone who is special in my life, too many to name but you are probably in this book anyway. A big think you to my whale Lee, I love you past the stars and none of this would have been possible without you.

My boys.. ..you can read this when you are 40 and I hope I make you as proud as you make me.
Big love.
xxx

MY 1ST DYSLEXIC DIARY

By
E R MARSHALL

Chapters:

My 1st dyslexic diary.

Chapter one

About ,Me and apologies

What the heck is this book about I hear you ask
yourself. Well I'm currently on maternity leave
after having my 6th son and my partner has gone
back to work full time having previously taken
time off to become an author (he has 6 books
available) so the tables have well and truly
turned and I'm the stay at home parent
attempting to be an author.

Unlike my other half I am not particularly
inventive and I have no idea how to actually
write a book so I figured I will just write about
me and things that have happened or stuff that
goes on in my head. So here it is my attempt at
being an author.
A little bit about me my name is Elizabeth Rose
Marshall , formerly Elizabeth Rebecca Hill,
Elizabeth Rebecca George and Elizabeth Rebecca
Page we will get into that later.

 I answer to many different abbreviations of my
name mainly get called mummy.

My other half Lee calls me Beth and so do his family, most of my friends call me Lilly, at work I am Elizabeth and even though I've asked them a million times not to my family and first husband call me Liz.

You might have already noticed that I am dyslexic so if you are easily annoyed with grammatical and spelling errors that you may want to stop reading or just enjoy being irritated for this entire book as I've decided to not have it professionally edited or proof read because this is me and I don't really make any apologies for it.

As I will be telling stories about my life you may think that I have mentioned you or things that have happened with you or people that you may know. If you are unhappy about anything I have said about you maybe you need to think about your actions or just pretend that I have changed names of characters in this book.

I don't have any intentions on making anything up or lying in this book but I may have accidentally fabricated some stuff for my own entertainment. Or just to make myself sound a little bit more interesting.

This chapter will mainly be used for me getting into the swing of writing I'll probably repeat myself a few times and ramble a lot as I do so feel free to bypass this chapter straight onto chapter number 2 which will hopefully be better. The idea of this book is that you can read just 1 chapter ,2 chapters ,read all of them if you like , but it doesn't matter what order you read stuff in particularly.

It's like I had bothered to keep a diary and I have copied and pasted all the good bits. I'm not putting any of the bad things in because you probably don't want to read it and I definitely have no interest in writing it. I wright how I talk. I waffle, I say fuck a lot and I will take the scenic route rather than just getting to the point. I think this is a good point to quickly say sorry to my parents and to avoid any more disappointment they should stop reading now. My mum is an avid member of the grammar police and my dad won't won't to hear about my sex life and other stuff I have been up to.

I was a devil child and a rebel teen and currently a mess of an adult- child. I'm very sorry about all of that and just remember that you are very good parents and I love you very much.

My brother and sister turned out great so you can tell people I'm adopted 9i used to wish I was adopted, not because I didn't like my family but because I had seen the film Annie too many times) or you found me under a bush on prom night , I will go along with it, that's the sort of thoughtful daughter I am.

If you are any member of my family it's probably for the best if we just deny all knowledge of this book to any other or your friends and extended family members too. That's that sorted…. Now to crack on….

I have been legally married and legally divorced twice, I have been engaged 3 times but proposed to 12 times, that's confusing maths.
 I'm currently married in the pagan sense (we had a beautiful hand fasting) though I consider that the most married you could be, Lee wants to do the legal bit at some point and I feel I should let him make an honest woman of me.
I'm sure that I will talk about that later.

My first marriage lasted 7 years and we had two boys, my second marriage lasted 8 years and we had two boys ,my third and current marriage is 4 years and going strong , we have a son together . I've had a few relationships and one son in between that ,again confusing maths.

As I write this my boys are 17, 14 ,10, 9, 7 and 4 months old. I am 35 and my partner Lee is 48 yes that is an age gap of roughly 13 years but the only thing that really affects is that I get to take the mick out of him for being old and having more wrinkles than me and we can't really talk about things we used to watch on TV as children, because I don't think TV had been invented when he was a child and as my children often say rainbows were in black and white when he was little!

I'm currently on maternity leave from a job I both love and hate , working alongside social services in children's homes.
Working full-time as a mother gives you such enormous guilt, you are so proud of the fact that you are supplying a decent wage for the household but you are never really at home long enough to enjoy the money with them. I would often work 80+ hrs a week.

Along with this you have all the social pressures ,like if you work at all then you are only a part-time parent and if you don't work then you're basically useless. You literally can't win with anyone so just do what works for you and hope your kids don't have attachment issues and meet therapy later!

I'm a bit worried about the idea of going back to work next year I'm currently breastfeeding so that would be an issue. (I would love to take Alfred to work with me but this is not an option).

And also it's hugely different leaving a one year old for a 72hr shift, than leaving a seven-year-old. when I say leaving I mean that leaving them with my other half not just leaving them in the garden attach to the rotary line ,with a bucket of gruel.

But now that Lee has a full time job I might not financially have to go back. But I do really want to go back to work even if it's just to do something part time or from home, I've never not worked at all and it would feel strange to be jobless.

Unless this book is a global success then I could just do this..... you know writing stuff. Hint hint, I'm sure this book could have many uses, for example propping up a coffee table or other wonky furniture.

It would make an excellent secret Santa present for people that you both like and dislike. Of course you could actually read it, and then recommend it to a friend or family member or anybody else that you know that can read and is over the age of 18 because I can't guarantee that they aren't gonna be some swear words and other over 18 type stuff.

It is sort of weird that I am even writing a book, mainly for the fact that I don't particularly like reading or writing and part of being dyslexic means that I'm not very good at either.
But I'm certainly not stupid and I would like to think that I could give other dyslexic people a glimmer of hope that literally anything is possible.

I am going to be telling some stories about things that happened when I was little, a teenager and older and some other stuff and mainly ranting as everything pisses me off as I have gotten older. From about the age of 30 everything is so annoying , people are annoying, animals are annoying and definitely the weather is annoying, why is it always too hot or too cold or too wet, it's like goldilocks and the 3 dam bears but it's only ever 'just right' about 3 days a year and all of them are in the autumn.

For this reason therefore my general annoyance I am allocating a whole chapter on my opinions and rants.

As I previously mentioned I am not good at making stuff up or lying so if I offend anybody by telling the world stuff I'm sort of sorry but sort of not because it probably did actually happen. And people should be accountable for their own shit.

I consider myself a relatively likeable person as long as first impressions don't count I'm more of a 'once you've spent a little bit of time with me you tend to like me person'. I know that I'm a good person in fact I pride myself on it I'm more charitable the most and I am the sort of person that would give my last one pound coin to a homeless person and walk home rather than taking the bus.

That actually happened to me once and I was heavily pregnant at the time and it was raining, one of those decisions that I kind of regret to be honest I'm sure that homeless person was going to spend that £1 on alcohol or drugs and I really could have done with getting the bus instead of walking but hindsight is a wonderful thing.

Even if you already know me I would like to think by reading this book you will know me a little better and if you don't know me I would like to think after reading this book you will!
A little bit about me – I like cooking, I like karaoke, I like my boys and my partner most of the time. I have a small handful of close friends and a large amount of other people I know that on occasion I call my friends.

I am tall , I think 5ft7 this just means I can't pick up just any trousers and all skirts are unintentionally short on me, I'm taller than Lee in flats and he refuses to go out in heels!
I have blonde hair most of the time but like to mix it up a bit just to confuse people.

My son Brody would often draw pictures of me when he was at nursery with a bald head, this was so he could add the hair at a later date once he remembered what colour it is. This resulted in about a year's worth of bald mummy pictures as he never got round to adding the hair.

He did also once draw me as a big boob with a head and legs, this is surprisingly accurate.

I sing every day, normally when I'm doing my makeup. About 5years ago I did x factor, it was on my bucket list (I don't actually have a bucket list but if I did it would have been on it) so I did it, I did ok (I had to leave half way through the 3rd round as Josh was in hospital)but would never do it again,
I found it very stressful and not good from my anxiety. ..

I have glasses , these are in fact corrective eye ear and I would like to get laser eye surgery at some point.
This reminds me of when my sister once asked to borrow my glasses as she was to be attending a "Where's Wally" fancy dress hen party,
I did have to point out the glasses on my face are actual glasses and I need them to see and I was quite baffled that she thought that I wore these glasses as some kind of fashion statement!

I found out about 6 months ago during a physiotherapy session that I have one leg longer than the other.
It's not quite bad enough to need an orthopaedic shoe but I am supposed to wear this little wedge of felt in one of my shoes.
... I don't often wear it and I don't walk around in circles so it can't be that bad.
I do however have moderate hip pain so maybe I should reconsider my options.

I won't leave the house without wearing a little bit of makeup especially my eyebrows that's because I don't really have much in the way of my own eyebrows due to over plucking in the 90s and I sort of look like a potato without eyebrows. If I do my eyebrows in a hurry I sometimes spend the day looking confused or angry!

My nails grow at a fast rate so I normally have quite long fingernails , the hair on my head grows at a much slower rate than average but the rest of my body seems to grow faster than average so that's shit, but that feeds my hot wax obsession nicely!
I do love pulling off a strip of wax and holding it up to the light to see the delightful hedgehog of pubic hair, simple things like this in life make me so happy.
I never really considered myself a picky eater but that's because I have spent so long feeding myself it wasn't until more recently when a friend invited me round for lunch and ask me if there's anything that I didn't eat then I realised that actually that list is quite

I think that's all the major pointless information about myself the other bits will be covered in the rest of the book, I hope you enjoy it.

Chapter 2

mini me

What's your earliest memory ? mine is ridiculously early, I remember things from being around 6 months old, at least I'm pretty sure that I remember. my parents have confirmed that at least of these memories are definitely true!

I remember being in my bouncy chair I remember the feel of the Waffle material with the pink ,yellow and blue bunnies on the cream background.

We had a golden Labrador called Lloyd who I would make noises at that so he would bounce me in my chair.
He was quite protective over the children in the family (ore so I remember my dad saying) but used to annoy a lot of the adults because he wouldn't let anybody go to the toilet by themselves and I can imagine it's quite unnerving having a large male adult Labrador dog staring at you whilst trying to pee.

My dad used to hold us on his back and let us go for doggy rides around the garden I remember being about 2 and running in and out of the paddling pool splashing the dog and him chasing after me nipping my bum.

He was a stupid dog ,he loved water and he certainly made use of the pet insurance, not because he injured himself or others ,but he would do things to cause other damage like when he crashed through the garden fence and ate the neighbour's designer curtains hanging on the washing line.

We would take him for long walks in Felixstowe but he would do the whole length of Felixstowe in the sea and we would have to take a smelly wet dog back home in the car.

Having three children under the age of 5 and the dog I think was a bit much for my hard working parents so they re-homed Loyd to a family that lived in Felixstowe or at least that's what they told us maybe he died I'm not too sure.

As an adult I found out that I am actually allergic to labradors ,that's sad because I kind of wanted one, in fact I did have one for a few months and that's how I found out that I am allergic to labradors to the point of severe asthma attacks and almost dying. Sounds dramatic but absolutely true.

Although not academically intelligent I'm pretty sure that I had a very well developed brain/mind from a young age.

You know when your baby or when a toddler is looking at you and you think to yourself "you know exactly what I'm talking about don't you, your just pretending to be stupid" , that may in fact be true.

Let me give you a few examples of why I think this.

My mum used to run the Sunday school at our family Parish Church, I often got the short straw out of me my brother and sister and had to go with my mum to "help out".

and I remember thinking what a load of shit! One time my mum was going to be decorating digestive biscuits with the children in the Sunday school as an activity she had planned. This was supposed to involve icing sugar mixed with water to create a runny icing put on top of the digestive biscuits and then adorned with little sweets and other edible items, my favorite being jelly diamonds.
(Can you even still get jelly diamonds or are they somehow obsolete?)

Anyway I distinctly remember going into the church hall with my mum and her bag of goodies to decorate the biscuits and her quite obviously wanting to get me out the way so she could have a natter with some old lady over a cup of tea.

I will point out I was about 3 maybe 4 years old at the time.

And as my mum passed me the bowl of icing sugar with the little jug of water and asked me to mix the two together to be very helpful big girl I remember thinking in my mind.... fuck you absolutely fuck you, you just want to talk to that old lady and ignore me and this isn't even a hard big girl job
,this is just to get me out of the way, fuck you.
....Or whatever the three year old inner monologue equivalent to fuck you is ,
because I don't think I would have actually have known the word fuck.

So do you know what I did ?????I made that icing ....I made that icing real good and I was giving my mother a very stern side eye. And the second she turned her back I took the spoon and ate it ,I ate all of the icing every last drop of it.
I managed to scoff nearly all of the jelly diamonds before I got caught too. Ha ha ha, in your face mother. Now not only gonna have to try and entertain a handful of children with digestive biscuits and no way of sticking any sweets on top them but also a very hyperactive sugar laden toddler hahaha.

I don't remember much more of that day I was probably in the sugar coma somewhere. But it was just perfect because what did you expect leaving a young child with icing sugar and sweets what did you expect to happen that will teach you for ignoring me and talking to that old lady in the boring Old Church that smells funny.

In hindsight I feel a little bit bad about that story because my mum bless her spent years and years volunteering it that Sunday school with little to no thanks in return and I was basically a shit!

My grandparents on my mum's side I call the apples on account of their surname is Smith so my granny is Granny Smith!

They did a lot for us when we were kids many times went swimming in Felixstowe at the leisure centre and my grandparents would take us to Pleasurewood Hills ib the summer and do what they could to relieve my mum and dad on the weekends. I take my hat off to you all because I know I was a handful.

I might have ADHD or something I don't know but I was definitely a pain in the arse.
We went to the zoo as a family once I think it was London Zoo.

I definitely remember sitting in the buggy for most of the time so I must have been about 2 , I think my mum was pregnant with my brother. The elephants squirted up some dirty stinky water and squared to do it all over the apples and my sister and everyone's spent the whole day complaining about how much they smelled.

I remember finding this quite funny and also being desperate to see the monkeys throwing their poop (that I overheard my granddad telling my mum about.) But no I didn't get too see the shit slinging monkeys that day but don't worry I have seen them now and so have my children

.

Looking back at some of the things I did as a child I was a definitely was a psychopath in the making although I have seen a therapist and I don't think I am a psychopath.

I was only 3 years old when I smashed my parents greenhouse not just the odd window but the whole entire thing.
I used my red plastic spade to smash the lower panes of glass and the ones I couldn't reach I just threw rocks at.
I had Thomas round to play at the time and the poor boy stood behind me and watched with snot dripping from his nose as it often did.

The sound of the glass breaking ….I still remember it now …..it was just so satisfying.

I think it was the neighbours that alerted my mum to her demon child trashing the place. The look of my mum's face as she came into the garden seeing me grinning away and all the broken glass everywhere and Thomas still stood there, nose still dripping.

I don't think I've ever seen my mum go so white so quick. But you know what neither me or Thomas had a single scratch on us I think it's some sort of miracle. (probably not an act of god) My mum was a decent mixture of angry and shocked.

But you can't really tell-off a couple of 3 year olds that you left unattended in a garden with a vast amount of glass, albeit you probably didn't think that you're demon child with smash an entire greenhouse.

It took my dad ages to clean it all up, he left the metal frame standing for a long time.
Somewhere my mum has a photo of me and Thomas swapping dummies, his dummy that's about to go in my mouth and had a long train of snot from his nose to the end of the dummy. Disgusting but cute.

We didn't stay in that house long, my parents were having a house built next door for us to move into.

I would often wonder over to talk to the builders and I would tell them stories.

Thinking about it they must have really hated me because they were actually trying to build a house and they had a 3 year old telling them about the haircut she gave her Barbie doll or the greenhouse 'someone' smashed!

I used to tell a lot of stories to people.
I used to embarrass my parents at nursery, I told the lady who ran it that my mum run over a cat....that we went in a hot air balloon and my dad will my mum's underwear.!!!!!

I have to explain why this is particularly funny, my dad is 6ft 6 and my mum is about 5ft 5 so the idea of my dad in my mum's underwear is funny at the best of times. And impossible.

It turns out I was very convincing with my stories as a 3 year old and my nursery teacher didn't know whether I was telling the truth or not.

It wasn't until she actually met my dad and realized the vast size difference between my mother and father that this must have just been me telling tales and when the teacher confronted my mum about the things I was saying they both became suitably embarrassed at the realization of my lies.

I had apparently gone into great detail about the knickers being pink and frilly and my dad wearing them with his work shirt around the house, much like a scene from a Freddie Mercury music video.

I can see where a lot of my stories come from (not the knickers story), my grandparents used to buy us those personalised books where you just had your children's names put into it and you go on great Adventures.

I'm pretty sure I was convinced that by the time I was four the books were based on actual events and so I of course wanted to share these stories with anybody that would listen.

 But looking back I don't know how convincing it would have been that a three-year-old could have single handedly piloted a hot air balloon or lead the circus through the town as a ringmaster. If nothing thing else I'm sure I re told the stories with great passion.

My brother joined edelweiss nursery when he was old enough and I distinctly remember me being put in the naughty chair ,which was a plastic chair in the toilets.... on my birthday! All because of him.... That's right on my actual birthday.
Whenever it was your birthday at the nursery everyone sang you happy birthday and they had a fake cake with a real candle ....
..my brother the actual shit blew out my birthday candle.
What a horrible thing to do...
. so as any normal child would...
 I bit him. I
 bit the shit really fucking hard right in the arm, he cried.!!! What a wimp, it didn't even bleed.
So there I was having to sit on the horrible piss smelling naughty chair on my birthday.

I remember questioning at where the justice is in this was but apparently though he did wrong by blowing it the candle out of my cake but I gave him his punishment when I left teeth marks in his arm.

I got my brother in into loads of trouble when we were little I once posted sticks in the cassette player of my mum's car and told her it was my brother.

I pulled the heads off my sisters dolls and blamed James.

Every poo left in the loo until about the age of 8 I blamed on my brother (I used to be scared off the sound of the loo flushing)
and it was definitely more likely to be my little brother leaving the offending poo ,so that was super easy to blame him.

We were both guilty for spinning the cat on dad's office chair and that was super funny till mum had to take the cat to the vet to find out why it kept being sick.

Me ,my brother and sister used to play a game called eat sock ,it does what it says on the tin.
 It basically involved getting one of my brother's dirty, smelly socks and trying to get the other sibling to eat it by shoving it in their mouth quite aggressively., often having to pinch the other child,s nose to get them to open their mouth to get the sock in.

We played other family friendly games, for example one of my personal favorites we played the game called 'funerals', this is where you had to lay on the floor and your siblings had to stand around you and pretend you are dead and say nice things about you.

But me and my brother would only say horrible things about my sister in this would make her cry, apparently for her not a fun part of the game!

Another fun game is where we would get inside our duvet covers and take it in turns to pull each other down the stairs in them ,we called this 'magic carpet rides', it actually really hurt and kind of fucked up the carpet on the stairs so didn't impress our parents (please dont try it at home).

My game (that I invented) that were used to play was swapsies, this sounds like an Innocent game right, almost educational some might say!!!
With a potential of learning such skills as haggling maybe even maths. ….
.. (wrong) …

So we would go into each others bedrooms take a collection of toys that we were interested in ….and then all meet in my sisters room as she had the biggest room .
We would then see what kind of deals we could cut with each other in our game of swapsies.

The first thing that would happen is my sister would basically say that she didn't want any of our stuff because it was all childish rubbish and that she wasn't willing to part with any of her things so she was quickly out of the game (she was smart).
My brother however , a vulnerable idiot.
(To this very day I sleep with a teddy bear that I fondly call Stinky bear that was bought for him as a baby, nabbed myself that bad boy years ago).

If ever my brother got a five-pound note for his birthday I would convince him that the family were trying to fool him with rubbish paper and I would give him a handful of my shiniest coppers as a swap, he was so happy!!! I would guess I owe him about £25.....

I'm pretty sure I still have my brother's Game Boy somewhere along with many of his cool toys such as 'he man' and ThunderCats. Figures....
Snooze you lose sucker.
Me and Roxanne once got a packet of refreshers and a couple of Kinder eggs,
we separated the refreshers into colours ,
chewed them up then spat them into the Kinder Egg plastic packaging and convinced my brother it was a delicious new drink!

Yes I do realise that is disgusting, but he was my little brother what was I supposed to do. He drank it and liked it so its not all bad.

My mum went back to work when I was about 6 months old and between my grandparents my next door neighbor Ellen and the nursery childcare was covered.

Ellen who is now 86 years old and a good family friend was the first person to take me to the cinema as a child ....we went to see Bambi.

I was clearly a delightful child and a pleasure to be with.... but quiet and demure were not parts of my character.. The part of the film where most people were having an emotional moment was when Bambi's mother died ....
where as I shouted out in the middle of the cinema while standing can we see the body!

Also during the film i loudly announced I needed the toilet and on my return from the toilet told everybody proudly that I had done a poo!

What an absolute treasure i was.

Ellen would often take me out on her bike, either sitting me in the basket on her seat as she pushed it along the path.

She would take me to the local farm shop and one time I got very excited that somebody had ordered half a pig and I wanted to see which half but Ellen removed me from the farm shop so I didn't to see the pig corpse.

There used to be a shop on the corner of lattice Avenue, it's now a house . Ellen would often take me to buy some penny sweets as a treat, I didn't
particularly like the sweets and took much greater pleasure in feeding them to Ellen's elderly dog called Tiffy
....who would go completely mental and a bit bitey from the sugar.
Tiffy once bit my brother's friend Roger after I had given her a glut of sweets,
I plan to take no responsibility for the dogs actions that day and considered it natural selection because Rodger was quite a weird kid and a bit of an asshole.
Often wonder what happened to him ... I haven't seen him for probably about 25 years.
 He has some very distinguishing scars on his arm left from the dog so would be easily recognisable .

When my brother was born Ellen came to the hospital to see him .. the midwife at the door told her the only family where allowed to see my mum (and brother) at that point and Ellen proclaimed that she was family.

The midwife clearly couldn't be bothered with the any sort of argument at this point because Ellen is anglo-indian and the wrong skin colour to actually be family but she let her in anyway.

I was about 15 until I realised that she was actually anglo-indian I guess as a child you don't see people for the colour of their skin she just was family to me.
She makes a great samosa too.
As a little girl I wanted to be a nurse ,Ellen used to be a nurse and she made me a miniature old style nurse's uniform and once took me to have lunch in the canteen with the real nurses at the hospital,
I was quite convinced that they would accept me as their own and not question the fact I was 6 years old.

I joined the st. John Ambulance as a badger ,not the animal that's what they called the youngsters at st. John Ambulance.

I think they were probably called badgers because we wore black and white , no after the animal because the actual animal badger is really are quite vicious and horrible, and not known for their lifesaving skills.

I was all up for being a nurse and was actually quite good at putting bandages on and doing the recovery position and stuff.

 As I got older I became to realise I wasn't really a fan of the sight of blood and unfortunately sometimes people died and you can't save everybody, so that put me off being a nurse.
 So the time and money spent on uniforms, trips and giving me a lift too and from st. John Ambulance headquarters
was a complete waste of time sorry parents.
Maybe had I have learnt of mortality at a younger age it wouldn't have been an issue!

I went to Noah's Ark pre school for a while before going to primary school and this is where I met my friend Roxanne ,she remembers me for going around trying to bite people with my crocodile gloves.
A bit of a legend if you ask me if you ask other people probably quite annoying.

I remember us having to make a man out of newspaper and old clothes ready to put on the fire for Bonfire Night.
As an adult I'm fully aware of the whole Guy Fawkes thing and the tradition of putting the guy on the flames and watching him burn.

Roxanne as a child found this very traumatic and wanted to try and save the newspaper man from his fiery death.... me is quite obviously a psychopathic child was looking forward to watching this paper man burn.
But as a loyal friend Roxanne I to pretended to be devastated.
Thinking about it , it is quite weird encouraging children to watch a man burn and celebrating his death.

Let's talk Father Christmas, my sister told me a very young age that he wasn't real but I continued to Believe in Father Christmas for a little while longer because I really needed the facts for myself and I thought if I stop believing I stop getting presents.

We had the beautiful family tradition of hanging Stockings at the end of our bed.... but my parents who for intelligent people are clearly not that smart because our stockings had bells on them.
 actual loud child waking bells,.

so at the age of about 5 of course I get woken up to my dad putting gifts in my stockings .
What the fuck!!!!

 was everything that I have ever been told about everything a lie!????

Then everything goes through your head ......is the tooth fairy real ????what about the Easter Bunny?????
if I swallow chewing gum will it really wrap around my heart and I'll die.

 What other bullshit is my parents were telling me ,to make me do stuff that I didn't want to do or be good ....when I didn't want to be good..... what is up with this bribery.

Obviously now I am a parent I realised that parenting is at least 30% about bribery.

 I had all kinds of mental images of my dad prancing around on the stairs wearing a tutu being the tooth fairy, and let's be honest I never really got my head around a bunny rabbit laying chocolate eggs to celebrate Jesus rising from the dead as a zombie.

But seriously it's you..... are you fucking kidding me... all the you made me sit on some old smelly man's knee and tell him what I want him to bring me at Christmas!

 If you have told me the truth from the beginning again would have been a lot less terrifying.

I never particularly like the idea of that old smelly man coming into my room as I'm asleep. I couldn't give a flying badger whether he has gifts for me or not.

Even though temporarily my dreams were shattered at the image of my father filling up my Christmas stocking by the morning I had worked it all out and felt much better about the situation. Then as you get a bit older you have the realisation that you can basically be an arsehole and your parents still have the buy you Christmas presents or they look like the arsehole to their friends hahaha.

I went to st. Johns Primary School this was a Christian school and my mum was a teacher at said school.

Fucking great! I never actually had my mum as my class teacher but she did make me write lines once for forgetting my trainers which I feel pretty sure as a 7 year old is her job!

I think I was a member of every after-school club and once won chess tournament just by making the other players surrender because I didn't actually know how to play.
At chess club a boy called Matthew had a really upset stomach once and had clearly shit his pants he sat on every chair before he realised that the shit on the chairs was coming from him! This was not an easy thing for him to live down.

 We all called him dingdong and even made up a song that went something along the lines of "ding dong, ding dong your bum smells strong"! What horrible little Christian children we were.

I have some other fond memories of primary school I remember when a girl in m y class Emily fell off the log and got amnesia and thought that she was Roxanne and Amy was her mother, (other girls in our class) I'm pretty sure she did make a full recovery.

Gemma was the first girl in my class to get pubic hair ,so we all wanted to have a good look and I remember it was like a proper Jackson 5 afro going on down there, where as I had maybe so much as a squashed spider of pubes.

This was the first and only time I have been jealous of pubic hair ,I have to say ever since they have been somewhat of an inconvenience.

Lucy was the first to get boobs and whowe also convinced so it was a good idea to pee in the corner of the outdoor changing rooms of the swimming pool.

Lucy was always teacher's pet, such a pretty little girl with her dark curly hair and big blue eyes, she always got the best parts in the school plays and the popular boyfriends......bitch.
But one lunch time I got to marry Nick and it was you having to chuck the blossom from the trees as our confetti as you looked on jealously and I thought .....in your face.

I actually really loved Primary School every bit of it. Our class that was something made of Legends , the sort of thing that you see in films. We had everything ,we had funny kids, fat kids, pretty kids ,geek kids , we had the lot ...we ticked every one of the boxes.

My Close friendship group consisted of me Hannah, kerry, Lucy and Lindsay. Then in Year 6 Roxanne was added to the mix. For years me Hannah ,Lucy and karry basically lived around each other's houses. I loved all their families as my own. Even argued with their brothers and sisters with them.

Being a child of the 80s was fantastic because it was before all the scary things were invented like the internet, paedophiles and germs!
We played outside till it got dark and drank out the hose when it was hot.

We took sweets from strangers and Jim fixed it!!!
Other thing about the 80s I loved- snap bracelets, troll dolls, my little pony and push pops, leg warmers, perms and WHAM.
Lucy had the best collection of troll dolls and I think I got her one for her 21st in a memory of them.

Me and Roxanne shared a diary for years it mainly consisted of which boy's we fancied, words we liked (bob, sid, poo and fart on the list) and on one page there is a squashed bug, circled with a small Remembrance note in it we called him c'heese Bob'. I still have this diary and my memory bag! I must go through it with Roxanne, its worth a trip down memory lane and she only lives around the corner.

When we were around 9 or 10 years old possibly 11 some of the girls had started their periods. we soon found out which ones "had really" started their periods and which ones hadn't ,because the ones that hadn't were busy putting different things on sanitary towels (for example pen or nail varnish) and the ones that had started their periods were very easily spotting out the fake menstruation.

Everyone became these period blood detective inspectors.

I personally drew the line at sniffing pads I really didn't care that much, some of the girls were getting quite passionate about it I'm surprised that they don't do this day have fanny blood detector on their CV!

I was a Tampax tampon girl myself so was not every a part of the pad police.

my mum got me my first thing and crop top set from m&s that had pigs on it, that's rather a random thing to remember I guess but I do remember the most random stuff.

I have the ability to completely forget anything of any use, for example my times tables. 7x4.... not a fucking clue.....

well I could work it out but don't have it as a recall at all.

As far as education goes in my preteen years I remember very little, I no Henry VIII had six wives and erm hang on.... no it's gone.

School was fun ... I remember the Lords prayer , yep I can remember that, and most of the words to "All things bright and beautiful".

For a year 6 trip we went to Norfolk, it was my first time away from my parents for 5 days as it was the first time for the majority of the children in my class.

We all paired up as to who we were going to share our bunk beds with, but when we got there ,there was one single bed so I gave my bunk position up to Roxanne and took the single bed.

Our teacher is very impressed with my chivalrous act. But then sat on my bed every night to read us girls books each night, that was annoying.

One day took trip to walk along the beach and go and see the seals ,when we got back on the coach there was a horrific stink and everyone was trying to work out where it came from.

It turns out Patrick had found a dead rabbit and had taken it in his backpack with intention of taking it home as a souvenir.

He was the strange child but I admired is strange bravery!

On the last evening of the trip we had a mini disco and all of the boys and girls were pairing themselves off to have their first dances.

I can't remember why but we tried to pair Roxanne off with the headmaster, but she insisted that she wouldn't go anywhere near him and in her words because he had the underarm of a gorilla!

I was a vegetarian when I was younger ,it was partly because I cared about the animals and mostly because I didn't like the taste or texture of meat or fish.

Instead of my parents having to say that I was picky was easier to say I was vegetarian.
I was the first and only vegetarian it in my primary school which was amazing because I didn't have to eat the grey meat and I used to get a massive pot of cheesy mashed potatoes all to myself.

Being a vegetarian seem to confuse lots of my friends parents and my grandparents, I would find myself having many conversations about how ham , and the little sausages you get inn beans is not vegetarian, thank fuck people are more educated now.

Me and Roxanne decided to be Buddhist for a while again I think we were the only Buddhists in the Christian Primary School!
Shocking I know.... my sister took great pleasure in taking the piss out of us for wanting to be Buddhist but I did remind her that the fact that we didn't want any harm to come to any people or animals was probably a good thing.

But then she told us we would have to shave our heads and where orange and there was a possibility of being reincarnated as a dung beetle and all of a sudden Christianity and the prospects of heaven and unlimited ice-cream sounded much more favorable.
At this point I will add that I am today pagan and don't even like ice-cream .

I was extremely lucky as a child to be able to go abroad with my parents every year in the summer holidays, I was 6 months old when I first went abroad.

I was the most ungrateful child you can ever imagine ,and that having such lovely holidays was a massive pain in the bum for me.

I will at this point also point out that I have freckly ,fair skin and suffered terribly with sunstroke.

When I was 7 we were on holiday in Portugal when I collapsed on the beach and had a fit, (it could have been the sun or the sight of the blood when my dad head cut his hand)..... when I regained consciousness my brother was crying and I thought that was quite sweet of him but it turns out, it's just because I'm knocked his sandcastle over.

My brother and sister spent the rest of the holiday doing impressions of me fitting that was delightful!

I felt like shit the rest of the time we were on holiday.

I also got mistaken for a boy twice on this holiday! I guess I was a bit of a tomboy at the time I had short frizzy hair ,obviously didn't wear make-up and thought nothing of walking around the beach with just shorts on, on account of 7 year olds don't have breasts and like I said paedophiles weren't invented yet.

When we came back from that holiday my mum took me to the doctor's to ask if I had epilepsy on account of the fit that I had but it turns out I just really don't work well in the sun.

I lost my first tooth whilst on holiday with the family, because some child was spinning round in circles with his arms out and punched me in the face, that wasn't fun!!!

 You know those places you go on holiday where there are lots of cats ,kittens ,dogs, puppies
 ......you know just basic animals wandering around.
Well I was the child that used to try and hide them and take them back to the hotel room and hide them under the bed and feed them scraps from dinner, this did not make my parents happy.
 They kept going on about things like rabies and disease I think they were being very overdramatic.

Apparently the final straw is when you get stopped at customs with a live puppy in your suitcase.!!!

I can't say I have changed that is definitely something I would still do.

I was 10 when we went to Greece that was a lovely holiday ....not.

.... my brother kicked me so hard in the vagina I started my period (he wasnt aiming for my vagina, we were just kicking the crap out of each other)!!!

I got such bad sunburn I could actually push the fluid from one blister to the next.

I accidentally got drunk drinking half a bottle of water from the fridge (you know you always have wather in the fridge on holiday because you cant drink from the tap) .

.then realising it was ouzo (really strong alcohol)
.

Actually that part of the holiday was quite good, and to this day my drink of choice would be anything aniseed.

My pre teen years were good all in all, be can't really complain can you, you don't really have a worry in the world as a child.

The worst things that probably happened in my preteen years were the Invention of something called "sun in" this just some watered down bleach that you sprayed in your hair and sat out in the sun and it turned your hair a straw yellow colour with hints of green.

my mum and Hannah's mum were not happy about this at all.

It was sad when my great nan died (she was very old) and even sadder when my cat was put to sleep and the other cat was hit by a car.
My year 6 was the first to have SATs but also the first to have sex education so I guess you win some and you lose some.

I already knew about sex because my mum had got a book for my older sister and after she read it I did. Lots of long words I couldn't read but the anatomically correct drawings helped.

Before reading the book/ looking at the drawings I was pretty sure you could get pregnant one of two ways ....either sitting on a cabbage patch or licking the lid of yoghurt . I was indeed wrong about both .....but I figured that's where Cabbage Patch babies came from and also that's why they called it the lid of life !!! ,maybe advertisers should think about the way that children might interpret there adverts !

Other shit things..... Boys..... boys were just shit went they.
They don't get much better but you find a few appealing attributes that they have as you get older.

I never got to try a turkey twizzlers because of the whole vegetarian thing so I can't tell you whether there were a good or a bad thing, Jamie Oliver's seems to think they were really bad thing and I quite like Jamie Oliver so I'll go with that.

I know it's going to make me sound like an ungrateful spoilt little shitbag but I'm going to have to put holidays on the shit list.

I was about 8 or 9 when I was diagnosed with being dyslexia and I had to go to a special needs school every Tuesday lunchtime my granddad had to take me and to be honest all I learnt was my alphabet (I might of learnt more but if I did I don't know what it was)and I'm still dyslexic so that's on the shit list too.

The list of good stuff, soooooo much good stuff.
Being a kids is great.
Having a pink puffer jacket and wearing a candy necklace as actual jewellery is the stuff dreams are made off.

Discos, kiss chase and sleep over parties.
I had the best family and the best friends in the world and was very happy.

Let's have a throwback to some of the awesome food ,for example crispy pancakes, (the cheese ones), pickled onion Monster Munch which I feel sure used to individually be the size of my fist, absolutely everything had artificial flavours , colourings and all the good stuff that made you hyper.
 smash potato, party rings, sunny D, the Old recipe of Linda McCartney sausages which were epic.

The best weekends where when you have saved up £5 of pocket money , you could get the bus into town ,get a hamburger Happy Meal or for me portion of fries and a vanilla milkshake to dip your fries into it, you could go swimming at Crown Pools , buy yourself some room oils and a cuddly toy from 'thing me bobs' and still have plenty of change for some penny sweets at the local corner shop ready to take to a sleepover round your mates and watch a PG possibly a 13 rated film on video your mates dad had rented from blockbusters.

 Before the age of 10 I had seen Beetlejuice, pet cemetery and Chucky all good films but definitely not age appropriate.

Leaving primary school and entering High School definitely sucks donkey dick.

going from very small Christian primary school and then a very large mainstream high school was a shock.

I tried to pretend I went to different primary schools when people asked, this was in an attempt to not get beaten up for being a "Bible basher."

Instead people just presumed I was really stupid when I said I cannot remember the name of the primary school I went to. Or if I said I went to Britannia it would undoubtedly be to a person who actually went to Britannia school, and they would look at you and say "you didn't go to my school" so then you go back to looking stupid.

Hannah and Roxanne were in my form at high school, and I resigned myself to the fact that I needed to make some more friends real quick. Or hight school whould be shit.
The second week of High School a boy called James , who sat in front of me and my maths class and past of ruler backwards to me which he had written on " will you go out with me?" !,,
I added the word "YES" and passed it back!!
My tummy does flip flops and I feel a bit sick just thinking about that moment. (he is now married to a woman who is much better looking than me so he up graded) .

Yes I had kissed boys before some of them had even been fully consensual and not just in the game of kiss Chase.

But I now had a real boyfriend a high school boyfriend.

James's nickname was weasel to this day I don't know why, if anyone does know feel free to drop me a message , I'm not that hard to find on social media .We dated on and off 24 times (yes I counted) until we reached 13 years old and that takes us to my teen years.

Chapter 3

 Teen Years

13 and me and weasel had just ended our relationship for the 24th and final time and I was on off dating 3 different Matt's!

I had discovered the Invention of Wella hair mousse and my hair was an interesting shade of mahogany, and it washed out easily and leaked on everything , pillowcases, t-shirts ,school shirts, my skin you name it it was everywhere, I had also discovered padded bras.

 And I'm pretty sure I was going through what I should call my rebellious years ......I smoked, well short of.

We pinched Kelly's, Roxane's or Jane's mums fags.
I would make 1 fag last ages and learnt all the slang , going 2's , saving doss and if you were a smoking pro you could do an Irish waterfall.
 I tried but I just got smoke in my eye.

And then you have the times where you had dry lips and years cigarette would get stuck to your lip and that hurt like fuck when you pulled it off taking half your mouth with it but you had to style it out like a pro.

I have been this taqll since the age of 11 so of course I was the chosen one to attempt to get served, it did actually work I have never been denied buying cigarettes ,we were posh we smoke Benson and Hedges , and you could get a pack of 20 for about £4.80.

And the Wannabe entrepreneur in me would sell them at the youth club for 50p each.

The cheeky panda pop and a smoke round the corner of the school down vagina close (I don't remember the name of the close but we all called it vagina close) was a right of passage for every one at my school.

Smoking was definitely cool, if you smoked you automatically cool end of.

Now I think it's quite disgusting (I am the worst ex smoker) and so expensive you would probably have to take out a second mortgage to have a 20 a day habit.

At high school l was super lucky because I was a floater and I don't mean a turd that won't flush. I was friends with literally everybody I didn't necessarily fit into one specific group I wasn't a geek ,I wasn't a bully but I was friends with those in both groups.

I'm still to this day friends with a girl called Kelly who was probably in the geek group and I became friends with her because I stopped her being bullied (I am also friends with the bully).

I think most people remember me from high school as being funny or maybe the one whose parents had a swimming pool (that's always going to help you be popular).

Thereafter I decided that I was no longer a Christian and people didn't want to pick on me for being a Bible basher ,I settled into high school life really well.

I just loved it (not as much as primary school) I love to love high school , not the teachers or the lessons but I loved making friends and break time and bunking off.

Sorry Mum and Dad but bunking off it is part of why I loved school and I know I shouldn't off, ...I was really good at it. I don't think I actually went to school on a Thursday for a year , I had double chemistry with Mrs scratch and sniff and I was not willing to attend.

One of my best friends Lorraine live down copleston road this made it ideal for bunking off. We could go to registration then go round hers and watch Jerry Springer,

go back to school for afternoon registration bingo back to hers for an afternoon of Maury Povich and other chat shows on sky1.

Me and Jane once got caught walking out of the school and apparently telling the teacher that we both had a dentist appointment at the same time wasn't going to cut it so we had to go back to school.

Jane lived near the hospital and her mum worked at the hospital , if ever we bunked off around her house we would have to hide in the garden when her mum came home from work for lunch.

Other parts of my rebellion involved going to Great Yarmouth that when I should have been at school in a friends of friends stolen car. (did not know it was stolen at the time) And if I remember correctly Lorraine will remind me if I'm wrong but we met Danny's friends in Yarmouth which we fondly renamed the Addams Family!

Our boyfriends did try and cheuk us in the sea but we stopped them as that was going to be a little bit hard to explain to our parents why our school uniform was wet with seawater.

Could have been a lot worse could've done other naughty things or come home pregnant oh no wait that was Yet to Come...

Throughout my teenage years lots of my friends tried drugs ,mainly weed ,draw things like that but I can honestly say hand on heart even to this day I have never tried drugs.

Well obviously I've had cigarettes alcohol and Calpol but not illegal drugs.

 Yes they were passed around at every party. I didn't really see the appeal I personally found that it stinks and makes you 'mong out' or sick. I've always been a lightweight ,a couple of drinks and I am the life and soul of the party. I am more often than not sick out of my nose at some point ,but this is always into a toilet or bush.

Things that every teenager has done whilst they are drunk-
some sort of rubbish attempt of acrobatics my personal favourite being where I attempted to jump over A car.

What this actually is me running into the side of a parked car, shouting did I do it.

 When you fall off the curb jump back onto your feet with the arms in the air asking if everyone Is ok.

Then at the end of the night telling strangers that you love them and you will never let Them go.

Taping people in a phone box.

Making prank calls.

Most of my drunken antics were before I was even legally old enough to.

Me and a couple of friends almost got arrested for being drunk and Disorderly.
I vaguely remember trying to convince a police officer to let my friend Eddie wee in his hat because he was pregnant!
After some time they didn't let him we in the hat but they agreed we will probably just drunk stupid and slightly loud rather than actually disorderly and we weren't Arrested
... I was only ever brought home by the police once and that was just a misunderstanding.
I did not know that the lad driving the car I was in ,stole the car and was probably not legally driving on account of him being 15, but it's an easy mistake to make.

Coming to think of it I think I have been in three stolen cars in My life! I was not a part of stealing any of them and I did not know they were stolen until after I had been in them!!!! I'm not too sure that's a particularly good defense but it's true.

Me and Amelia were really horrible to our German teacher I think her name was Mrs dix, you can't have a last name that sounds like dick without us being horrible to you.

And had a maths teacher that looks about 12 called Mr Mac ,you can fully expect teenagers to draw a Big Mac on your chalkboard or sing Return of the Mac at you!!!!! Thinking about it now we were actually very horrible and I do regret it. … sorry....
I think we caused one of our R.E teachers to have a nervous breakdown, we would do things like turn her desk around so when she went to come in the classroom she couldn't open the drawers, or we would just repeat everything she said in whispers. …...I don't know what was worse being a slightly demonic toddler or a complete bitch of a teenager.

But wasn't all bad I used to go and do flower arranging at st. Elizabeth hospice after school for the terminally ill people, and I did that completely off my own back.... I wasnt good at it but I did try.

I got three detentions whilst at high school.
One was for calling my PE teacher a racist because she wouldn't let me wear black socks (the uniform was white socks). One was for handing in my art homework the late even though I tried to give it to my teacher the week before. (what a bitch)

And the other one was from my maths teacher for disrupting class even though I only clicked my pen.
I probably should have had a lot more detentions but I think a couple of the teachers were scared of me and the rest of the teachers I was scared of them.

We had one teacher that kept 2 bricks on his desk ,one would be a real break and one would be a sponge brick and you never know which one he was going to throw. and trust me he did a few times throw the real brick.
He once threatened put Max in the bin and Max said that "you would get fired if you did that" and he responded "but it would probably be worth it".

My mum's signature was really easy to fake as it's just her name written in super neat teacher writing. And when you're on your period for the 8th week in the row the PE teacher starts to get wise.

One time my hamster did actually eat my school jumper and my mum wrote a note but the teachers thought that I had faked it!
Yes kids the moral behind the story of the boy that Cried Wolf is a thing.
I wasn't predicted very good grades at school this was down to being dyslexic and also not doing any homework so they didn't really have a lot to base their predictions on.

If it was a class I enjoyed I was an active member ,but if I didn't like it or care about it and wasn't scared of the teacher I used it as a social gathering.

When it came to sitting my exams I was offered additional help but I figured I had got that far without any help I didn't want any special treatment in my exams.

I came away with 11 GCSEs 10 of which are grades A to C. Rather impressed myself with that. Although I was a bit of a shit at school I did revise hard where it counted so I didn't get good grades by chance.

Throughout my teenage years I still went to my apples (Grandparents) for dinner on a Tuesday night after school.
Granny would do the cooking, it would normally be a chicken casserole with vegetables grown by my grandad in the garden.
Grandad would wind us up if we asked for seconds of pudding because he would say that was his supper.

We knew he was winding us up but we entertained the idea ,giggling and going along with it as it had become some sort of tradition.
Granny would sometimes make a blancmange rabbit, with mashed up green Jelly for the grass and chocolate drops for the rabbits poop much to Granny's amusement!

Every damn week's my shit of a brother would make me be sick on the way home, be either punching me in the guts or making gagging sounds.

Me and James were pretty awful to each other during our teenage years but we were best of friends too.

We had each others backs we covered for each other with any sorts of contraband found by my parents, normally lighters.

together we would pick on Kate. We got our own back now that we were bigger and there was two of us we would get her to eat the sock. We were a formidable Force, eat sock reigning champions for a year.

Kate always wanted to watch MTV on the telly but me and James we had other ideas. Live and Kicking on a Saturday morning oh oh yes.

Watching Sabrina the Teenage Witch or sister Sister or Nickelodeon, hell yeah. I'm sure she hated us for a good few years and I don't really blame her.

I would still hang out with Lucy ,Roxanne ,Hannah and Kerry But we had all added new friends to the mix.

I went on a terrifying caravanning holiday with Kirsty and her family, I even phoned my mum asking to come home but they had gone on holiday without me!So I was stuck in a crap caravan with a terrifying group of people and no way of getting Home.

Maybe terrifying is a bit strong. But she did eat all my veggie food and take my money.
Our friendship was short lived.

I was friends with a lovely girl called holly, she showed me how to bleach my tash and I gave her a questionable perm!

We had some fun parties at Alisons House, most of which ended in partial nudity from playing truth or dare.

We had a lunchtime gang round Lorraine's house.

We should've worked out Robert was gay when he made us a lunchtime gang cake for our last lunchtime together!

I got my first tattoo of a butterfly on my hip when I was 14,(anyone that lives in Ipswich knows exactly where I would've got my tattoo from). It's like in Ipswich tradition …. everyone had a tattoo from him right.!!! Anyway I got this tattoo to commemorate me and Lucy singing in front of the whole year and doing some questionable Irish dancing.

If you get a couple of drinks on me I will show you my rubbish Irish dancing , it's got no better but that's probably because it couldn't get any worse.
I'm going to take this opportunity to talk about some of the legends that were in my year.

Amelia , not too sure why you're a legend but everyone knows who you are so I feel like you should get a mention.

Kenneth , you wrote in my yearbook 'goodbye from Kenn', I felt that you really meant that. For my birthday once offered to steal me some ethanol from the science lab. Thanx for that. Top lad.

Nathan he was one of those boys that you just knew he would do well for himself and I'm pretty sure that he has, yes I am jealous so that's all I'm going to say about that.

Michelle you were the 1st to have a baby in my year and believe you're going to be the first grandparent. All the best to you my love ,you seem like a lovely person. (harry tells me he is going to marry one of your girls)

There is really nobody I disliked at school , well not that I can remember anyway.

The first time I felt an erection… was an accident.
Me and one of the 3 Matt's were hanging out on the heath and having a snog in the bushes.
 I felt his pen digging in my hip.
I put my hand in his pocket to move the pen.......... it was not a pen.

That killed that moment and left us both suitably traumatised.

 The second time I felt an erection was at the zoo! Yes it was a human willy before you think I am a weirdo.
That too was an accident, accident might not be the right word.

Alison said that Ben looks like he has an erection, I said it was just his pen. She said she would bet me £1 it wasn't his pen.
 ....She won the pound coin and I yet again grabbed a cock not a pen!
I don't know if this proves my innocence or stupidity!

 Teen age boys are confusing…. Why would you have an erection at the zoo??
A pen made way more sense…..
Who can say the first 2 erections they ever felt were both not mistaken for as pens. …...Only me.

My mum and dad let me go to the pub to go to karaoke several nights a week from a very young age,

This wasn't irresponsible of my parents seeing as there was normally Kerry's mum there to supervisor us.

Well I say normally I mean sometimes …..no I don't I mean really I mean she came a couple of times. ….But we didn't drink or smoke, …..well not a lot anyway, …..ok we had Archers and lemonade or a lager and lime and we smoked a reasonable amount.

It was in the 90s where you could smoke in pubs. granted as 15 year olds we shouldn't have been in the pubs and certainly not drinking or smoking. But it kept us off the streets I guess.

We went to the Orchard on a Thursday and Sunday night, the case is altered on a Friday and Saturday, occasionally we would go to the Duke of York or the Rose and Crown.
Wherever kev was doing the karaoke, it's really funny to think that Kerry is now married to him with two children.!!!We had the best nights they were such a laugh.

As we got a bit older 15/16 maybe we started going to some of the clubs. .. dancing with boys and drinking more hooch and mad dog 20/20.

Had a couple of jobs in my teenage years I worked at Fatty Arbuckles as a waitress and then later in the dessert kitchen making the dessert and milkshakes.

Oh it was so much fun with Jez in the main kitchen and he would always get out too many stakes accidentally and I would always get out too many profiteroles and we would get steak , chips and profiteroles after our shift.... fabulous. Definitely worth working for minimum wage which I think at the time was maybe £4 an hour. for.

On Monday night after work we would go to liquid (night club) for 70s and 80s night wearing massive brightly coloured afro wigs.

We never invited our boss cos she was a twatt. I once got stuck in the walk-in fridge with one of the waiters who I sort of fancied called Pete. Unfortunately we were rescued before we had to cuddle up to keep warm.

Anybody that remembers Fatty Arbuckles remember the fatty challenge, if you completed the challenge, which was eating an obscene amount of food you would get a Polaroid picture taken and stuck on the board I think you got a t-shirt and your meal for free.

My dad did it once I think ,but he did all the ice cream in pint glasses underneath tables, ….Smart move father.

Another evening and weekend job I had was working in the call center for zenith windows, yes I was that annoying woman that phoned you up and tried to sell you double glazing just as you would served up your dinner.

We were given a script a few pages of the local phone book and given the rule that we were not allowed to end the phone call you had to wait until the other person ended it!
 Sad but true. It wasn't insanely boring job but I got to do it working alongside my mates, all we needed was to bring a couple of bags of sweets and a box of fags to get us through the shift.

 We will try and make the shift slightly more interesting by giving each other fake names to use for the shift ,I was often fanny or dave.
I hated that boss too, she was common as muck and called me Elizabuff…. meh.

She was a larger lady and once she was demonstrating how strong are windows were by standing on it and the window smashed …..it was funny, as fuck… she did not appreciate the stifled sniggers.

Oh please Karen do you show me how strong are windows are with your gargantuas weight you fat biffer.

Kramer was on my side that day. Don't shout at your staff if you want any sort of respect.

About two years after we finished working for Zenith and they was all new management we decided to go in for walk-in interviews and take it in turn to pretend we had Tourette's, that was a Saturday afternoon well spent.

 After the third one of us had shouted out "fudge packer" at the top of our lungs we were asked to leave.

That is something else I should probably apologise for ,but you know what I'm not going to.

I met Gary (my first husband) for the first time in ' the case is altered pub' I was 15, he dated two of my friends before he dated me.
We quickly fell in love or at least what we thought was Love at the time.

I was still at school and working part time, he had just left school and was doing an apprenticeship.

Being at school and having an older boyfriend with the car definitely made me even cooler than I was.
we spent every possible second together.
I think for the first year or so we hadn't been apart for longer than 16 hours.

We spent so much time together our friends nicknamed us Giz and Larry.

Our first kiss was the turn of the Millennium....
16 years old and at Kerry 's house party.
It most definitely wasn't romantic I had just been grabbed by a random clown (fancy dress clown) in the street who stuck his tongue in my mouth!

I spun round and Gary was stood at the bottom of the steps I said happy new year dude and he turned to kiss me.,
#
it was very awkward but that marked the start of our 7 year relationship.

Fast tracking it a bit .... By the time I was 18 we were engaged, pregnant and living in our first house that we had a substantial mortgage on!

This marks the end of my teen years....

Chapter 4

Adult-ish

I'm 35 and I still feel like I am just playing at being an adult. I still don't really know what I want to be when I grow up and I don't know how to act my age as I have never been this old before.

  Getting pregnant at 17 meant that I had to grow up pretty Dam quick. I was on the pill and using condoms but still managed to get pregnant. I
 am the most fertile person in the world, I'm sure I should sell my wee to put on prize winning Rose's or something.

 Now with 6 children 2 divorces, 2 dogs, 4 budgies and my best friend and life partner lee by my side I am adult-ish.

The first time I felt like an adult was at Joshua's first parents evening.
This was also the first time I was sat outside of a classroom not waiting to be told off.

But I still sat there with a slight cold sweat wringing my hands wondering what the teachers going to say to me.

The teacher just said positive things about Josh and I thought well I'm an actual real parent / adult, that day it really hit me for the first time.

Even though I had been a real adult for about 5 years and had two children it was that moment that I really felt it.

You can do some great things once you are an adult. You can still have pudding even if you don't eat all your main in a restaurant.
If you're cooking for yourself you don't even have to cook vegetables, that's just a parent thing to make your kids healthy and show off to other parents.

I can cross the road without holding anyone's had (but I should hold hands with a real adult if available).

I can say fuck and shit without losing my pocket money.

Kids think your smart and wise..,,, I did recently teach my four-year-old nephew that you have to let a baby smell the back of your hand before trying to touch them so that they didn't bite.

Because I am an adult he believed me…. Sucker.

There are many things that I do on a day-to-day basis which are classed as adult things but I still am not too sure that I'm doing it right and I think that I could use a real adult to show me how to do them properly.

For example, hanging washing to dry….. I don't know where the pegs should go.

I feel like a little girl hanging her dolls clothes out on the fake washing line and people are looking at me saying "oh look at that child doing it all wrong".

But it's not something they teach you in school. Another example, cooking g a roast dinner…. when you are a child ever y adult you know can cook a roast dinner. But you don't wake up on your 18th birthday with all this adult knowledge do you.

Parents should tell kids this. You actually have to learn this stuff and when I was 18 we didn't have the joy's of YouTube.

Now kids have it easy their is a YouTube video for literally everything.

Give me a couple of hours to watch a few videos on YouTube I could probably remove your appendix or make a working blow dart out of household items.

But no I had no such luxury had to wing it several times before I got the hang of it.

Now I am rather good at cooking a roast dinner I actually make the best roast potatoes in the world.

I know that they are the best in the world because my children told me so and children are stupid and not very good at lying.

I know that they have probably only tried about five different roast potatoes in their short lives so they can only really say that mine are the best out of the five different ones that they have tried but to them that's the whole world so I'll take it. Don't worry dad yours of the second best.

I have actually passed my theory test for my driving but I'm pretty sure I don't actually know how to read road signs.

Whenever I'm in a car I think to myself how did you know you should be in this lane or how did you know not to turn up there.

These are not inherent adult skills they are things that you need to learn.

My brain doesn't work like that, I still don't drive.

I can work a car but freak out when I am near other cars and that's a large part of driving.

I had a car for a while it was a Nissan Micra in oceanic blue and I called it Mike Wazowski, owning a car with a very adult thing to do it wasn't it.

Sitting in my car parked on a driveway making car noises was not!

After a year of owning the car and driving it only twice with my dad (that was an experience hey dad)....the car was sold.

I passed my cycling proficiency when I was at primary school but I'm still not very good at that either, the saying " it's just like riding a bike" is very apt for me but not for the reasons it's intended.

I often do things and think to myself yep this is just like riding a bike it looks pretty easy but is really not!

Something else is just like riding a bike tying shoelaces.... most of my adult shoes don't have shoelaces.... years without tying shoelaces then tried it, it was just like riding a bike ....not as easy as I remembered.

Shaving my leg, I don't think I have ever done them without taking a chunk of skin off my ankle, you don't even have hair on your ankles but I do it every time.

And its bleeds loads the bath looks like a scene from jaws.

And as we are in the subject of hair..... in my teen years I worried about a little peach fuzz on my top lip.

I hit 30 and I'm sure I could grow an actual beard.

I was watching the greatest showman with the kids and I felt I could relate to the bearded lady. In my head I sing "this is me" as I pluck my chin hairs.

Maybe I have polycystic ovaries,....I should see my dr.

I hate being a woman sometimes, bleeding every month sucks.

I always get killer cramps and have been known to pass out.
after reading many horror stories about tampons I decided to get myself a moon cup.

I was 32 and have given birth to 5 children.
Having done pelvic floor exercises every day for the last 14 + years I'm not a "bucket" so went for the smaller size.

So the day came when I was ready to try this bad boy out.

I read all 7 pages of instructions and examined the graphic pictures.

With copious amounts of lubrication and some gentle persuasion I managed to insert said cup. It did in fact feel like I had put one of the children's toy cars up myself or something.

I took a few lunges around the living room to try and manoeuvre it into a more comfortable position.

It didn't work so I tried to poke it up a little further (as recommend on page 6).

Still feeling like I was being stretched I tried to carry on about my day and went to work.

After a somewhat embarrassing lesbian photos shoot (me the photographer) I came home and was ready for the removal!

 So in the bathroom I stood with one foot on the toilet and completely naked from the waist down I prepared for extraction.

How the hell are you supposed to get a hold of a very small well lubricated 5mm nub of silicone!! Oh god it's stuck! I tried and tried to pinch the dam thing but the harder I tried the more frustrated I got and the more my pelvic floor decided to clam the moon cup as its own.

This tug of war went on for longer than I care to admit.

Who the hell do you call in this situation?
I was tempted to call Kat but she would of just laughed at me.

I wasn't willing to let a dr or fighter give it a go. So I sat on the loo and started my own removal method of giving birth to it.

I am proud to say with only 5 pushes and a little tug and no gas n air it plopped out into the loo, FREEDOM.

I don't think i have ever been so relieved.

I then inserted a tampon and vowed that I would never try such a thing again.

I will add that lots of my friends get on very well with a menstrual cup. It's just another adult thing I'm not good at.

I still have months where I am caught short and have to fashion myself a sanitary pad out of toilet roll. Please don't tell me I'm the only one that's done it.

Let's talk money and paying bills, first of all a huge proportion of my hard earned wages go on stuff that I don't really want but definitely need. Gas ,water , electric, council tax, mortgage and life insurance.

Having life insurance is a very adult thing. It means that once you have life insurance you're definitely worth more dead than alive. This is probably why we don't tell children about it because they would have us killed off. But if you don't pay your bills you get angry red adult letters.

I think it's a good thing I don't have "extra money " because I am a random shopper.

I could definitely find some way to justify a pet goat or glow in the dark trainers.

I do let myself spend £30 a month on random stuff. It's like adult pocket money.

Granted if I was a proper adult I wouldn't need a £30 a month budget to buy total shit.

It's become a little challenge, I like to show lee or the kids my random buys and have them shake their head at me in slight disappointment. I got myself a rug for a dolls house that was made from a taxidermy mouse.

I don't even have a dolls house so it makes for a slightly too chunky book mark.

I got some heart shaped sun glasses, I can't use them on account of needing prescription glasses and not being able to use contacts (I was told I don't blink enough).

I have myself a very cool yo-yo and a book to learn tricks! I haven't mastered making it go up and down yet but when I do you will all be so jealous.

I got pink tinted dog shampoo, but it didn't work on Nancy because she is almost black and leliu is a diva and won't let me bath her.

You would be amazed at the shit you can buy on the internet, a jar of toenail clippings was the most random.

I didn't buy it as I couldn't think of a use but it gave me an idea.

I gave lee one of my toe nails and a used plaster with a note saying 'if I die use the money from my Insurance and these items to Clone me" he didn't like the gift. …..

If this book sells well I will up my budget to £50 a month. Just think of the possibilities.

In my years of being an adult I have come across some adult hacks.
I will let you know some of them and this will undoubtedly make this book completely worthwhile buying-

Splinters, you don't need to dig around with needles or tweezers no no apply a piece of Sellotape pull the Sellotape off and splinter comes right out.

If you shake your phone whilst on Facebook or Instagram you can alert them of a problem, I only found that one out last week.

Whitening toothpaste can be used for loads of things, cleaning stuff, it can remove permanent marker from lino flooring or make the white rubber bit of the kids trainers white again. You can put toothpaste on spots and they shrink.

If you have an ice cream/ ice pop with a stick use a cupcake case to push the stick through to catch any drips to save sticky hands and sofa.

Tumble dryer everything and then put it straight onto hangers when it's still warm, it saves on ironing, ironing which is another adult thing that I'm not too sure I'm doing right.

Lemons are a wonder fruit, put half a lemon in your dishwasher and the other half in your fridge. Change it twice e a week, you an thank me later.

I can't think of any more adult hacks right now but I might add to this section later. ....
…..................
….......
…...........
…......

(got some more)
Walk to the gym and back and you won't have to join a gym. That's a really good hack.

If you can't be bothered to go upstairs to call the kids for dinner just turn the internet off and they appear as if my magic.

If you put a slice of bread underneath each chicken keiv when you cook it , it's soaks up all the garlic butter that comes out and you end up with a nice piece of garlIc bread.

Slow cookers…. Buy one , join some slow cooker social media groups and you are set for life.
…..........

By the time I was 18 I had done everything I should of waited till I was 18 to do.
 I have been drunk and had gotten tattoos and piercings.

That reminds me I forgot to tell you about the nipple piercing I got when I was at college because I lost a bet, don't make stupid bets with people.

So far in my life I have had 26 tattoos but the one on the pad of my finger washed off and the whale on the underside of my foot (that I tattooed myself but don't try it at home) gradually disappeared.

I had my tongue pierced twice but currently don't have it done.

My first holes in my ears were done at the purple shop much like every girl in the 90s in Ipswich.

I did the second hole myself with a thumbtack out off the wall in German class (don't try that at home, it hurt).

I had the top of my ear pierced and my tragus . Got my nose done for the second time last week. The first time I had my nose done it didn't last long because the stud fell out at work on a 48hr shift.

I did try and put a stud back in when I got home but that really fucking hurt and made my eyes water a lot so I just left it.

I would like more tattoos but they are expensive and lee banned me from using the tattoo gun I got off amazon!

He did say I could have it back when I grow up and use it responsibly, that should be any day now.

I remember watching quiz programs with my parents as a kid thinking that my parents must be geneses because they answered loads of questions and I didn't even understand the questions.

Now I take great pleasure in watching the chase with the kids... I know loads more of the answers than they do. Yay me.....

It's always slightly intimidating when you look around and realise that you are the responsible adult!!

I did have an experience where I had to pretend extra hard to be an adult... I got offered a long weekend job working in Benidorm as a make-up artist on a photo shoot.

I had to do adult things like getting on an aeroplane and making sure that I got to the right hotel and all adult stuff like that.

I was most definitely the odd one out on this all expenses paid working trip ,I was the only female member of the crew and the only other femals on the trip were models.

This meant that for the all-you-can-eat breakfast I was with the lads having carb on carb where as the females were drinking black coffee and smoking cigarettes for breakfast (this is not me stereotyping this is actually what happened).

On the Friday and Saturday night all of the lads went on to the square to watch half naked women, get fully naked.

The models got an early night to maintain their beauty ready for the next days photo shoot. Like a total legend I am, I found the only English pub in Benidorm called Queen Vic and did karaoke by myself.

The shoot on the Sunday morning was canceled due to weather, so this meant I had the last day or to myself.

I did what every self-respecting adult would do and took a bus to the local zoo/sea life centre. I wanted to get a picture of myself with a dolphin.

I see lots of people with selfies with dolphins where they are giving them a kiss on the nose or hugging them or something else that could be on the front of a post card.

But not me I wanted a photo of me trying to finger the dolphins blowhole.

I didn't want to hurt the dolphins I didn't wanna actually put my finger in its blowhole but it's really hard to explain to a Spanish person that you just wanted to mock a picture of fingering a dolphin is blowhole.

This ended in Spanish people shouting at me asking me to move my hand.

Unfortunately I did not manage to get the photo I was after ,but you can find on my social media picture with me with my hand on the dolphins back looking rather smug. (I did get asked to leave after this photo was taken)

Maybe I should put that on my bucket list to actually get the photo I was after.
I did also manage to buy some questionable gifts on the Spanish market.

I managed to get a moving, light up Father Christmas riding a reindeer that also played dodgy Christmas tunes, an anatomically correct baby boy doll, several pairs of most definitely fake trainers and some headphones , unfortunately this meant that I went over my baggage allowance and I had to pay £40 for the extra weight of my suitcase so I didn't save any money on my fake goods.

…...Adulting at its finest.

I'm looking forward to growing up one day. I can't wait to have grand babies. I will fill them full of sugar, shake them up and send them back. I will buy them drum kids for Christmas and let them cover their bodies in temporary tattoos.

Retirement sounds like fun, I don't have any real plans other than letting myself go disgracefully.

I will eat utter shit and go to the shops in my slippers.

Chapter 5
Sexy time

Let's get down to it. How old were you when you lost your V and how many have you been with???

Two really irrelevant questions if it's a man asking a man.

Most women lie if a man asks and is shy when a woman asks.

I don't really know why. It's also something that families definitely don't talk about or want to know.

I am happy in the knowledge that my mum has only had sex with my dad and that was just the 3 times in order to conceive me, my brother and sister.

My mum can be happy on the knowledge that I too have only had sex to conceive my children. And if you believe that you will believe anything!!!!!!

Why is it called the birds and the bees.

I don't think ether even have a willy or a mini do they?

I was never too sure how you should answer the the question when the children asked…. How do mummies get a baby in their tummies?????

And they always as at the most inconvenient times. The first time it was Harry that asked and he was 4, I was in COSTA so I was able to cause a diversion and offered him a chocolate chip muffin and he didn't push the subject again.

Josh was 10 when I sat him down to have "the talk". I decided to use an anatomically Correct approach, he looked at me with his head tilted to one side with very wide eyes.

When I got to the bit about the willy going in the special baby hole , Josh dramatically spat his juice out and scared the dog so bad she shit on the rug…..
could of gone better!

I haven't given "the talk" to any of my other children yet but when I do I will be making sure they have a mouth full off drink coz that was funny.

What about different places you can have sex, when you get to a certain age I think you can only do it in a bed.

I don't know what that age is, maybe 50… definitely 60???

I don't know but I haven't reached that age yet. I have ticked most boxes I think.

I'm not a member of the mile high club yet but I think have covered all other modes of transportation.

Other normal places like in a lift, in a public loo, phone box, friends bed, garden, field, tent, b and q….. tick tick and tick all of them.
 Then you have all the different areas in the house, in the bath, shower on the dinner table…. Never in the kids rooms because that's just not right.

The slight risk of getting caught is exciting ,but as you get older it becomes more nerve wracking than exciting, then you can experience performance anxiety and that's no ones friend.

I think the different names for sex mean different things.-

Sex is what you do to have a baby.

A quickie is under 5mins with no foreplay.

 A shag is what you do when you're young and it's not much more than itching a scratch.

Fuck is with lots of passion , ripping off clothes and pulling hair.

Making love is special, it's what old married couples do and what you do after a romantic candle Dinner, lots of soft kisses and snuggles.

Banging is a one night stand in an alleyway.

Porking is probably a chubby people thing.

I know people use lots of other words for it but they don't come into my vocabulary.

I have personally never had a one night stand and I can hand on hart say I had feelings for everyone bloke I have slept with (slept with.. means intercourse With a partner).

The majority of people I have slept with I have had a baby with, I don't know if that's a good thing or not.

I just don't understand why you would have a one night stand.

I would almost definitely end up pregnant or with syphilis no matter how careful I was.
I don't know if it's just me but sex is only amazing once you and your partner get to know what each other likes!

You would have to be very confident on a one night stand to be shouting directions,..... left a bit, slower, harder, pull this, bite that, call me Karen. Fuck knows.
Do you call the other person a cab?
Do you shower together or wait till you get home?
I have many questions. If you know me personally and you are someone that is partial to having sex with strangers I would love to go for a coffee so you can educate me.

I have met people that have had sex with over 100 people! How is that even possible? I don't think I even like 100 people let alone want to bang uglies with 100 people.

Where are you people finding the time for this and do you carry clean pants and a toothbrush around it you? Soooo many questions it's making my head hurt.

Feeling sexy is a massive thing. I haven't yet mastered the feeling of sexy from within.
But I'm not overly comfortable in my own skin.
I'm very relying on other people to help make me feel sexy.

 Lee is good at this and it's one of a billion reasons I love him.

I can wake up in the morning with my hair everywhere looking like Einstein and have the worst dogs bum morning breath and he will tell me he was watching me sleep (not in a creepy wants to make my skin into a coat so of way) but in a hurry up and wake up cos I want to fuck you coz your so sexy sort of way.

Or I will be watching Tv and he will just look and me and say "god you're sexy"
.he has that ability to make me blush.

Me and Kat did pole dancing classes once, we told people it was for finesses.

I might just be talking for myself but I wanted to be a sexy pussy cat doll or a female magic mike. First of all, I have the upper body strength of a newborn and I made pole dancing look like a fat greasy kid sliding down a fireman's pole at the park!

It was the least sexy thing you can think of.
Kat was shit at it too but she made it work for her and was definitely sexy.
Lou earnt every penny of his money in those classes , I can't fallow simple instructions, he must of said "Lilly try your other left" about 200 times before he just expected I get my left and right confused (it's a dyslexic thing).

I have a couple of embarrassing sex related stories so I might as well share them in a book that is available for anyone in the world to read! Because I am a great partner I decided to get a pop up pole (even after discovering I was useless at pole dancing), it's a tension set pole that's to dance around so you can do a sexy strip.

It says clearly in bold red writing THIS POLE IS NOT WEIGHT BEARING.

The child in me is very defiant and I will insist I know better than things like science or Government health Warning.
You can guess what happened but I will build a full image for you.

I put up the pole by the end of the bed, I gave it a good had tug and made sure it could take my weight.

 As long as I keep it to little slinky movements it will be ok (it was not ok).

So I gave lee a handful off Disney Monopoly money , put on some stripper music (I picked tainted Love so I could pelvic thrust to the beat). It sounds super sexy already hey.

I got myself a lace number from China, it took me 20mins to work out how to put it on but it was ideal for stripping paper money to be pocked into.

I told lee to brace himself and asked Siri to play my music.

I was doing it.. I was dancing, I was slinking round the pole like a sexual snake, dripping oil over my ample bust and flicking my hair about the place.

Lee was giggling at me, not the affect I was after so I upped my game and invoked my inner Carmen Electra.

I went to swing off the pole ,my oiled hand slipped and I feel spread eagle , head first into the bedside cabinet , knocked myself out then the pole fell and landed on top of me......

Half naked , out cold, monopoly money in my arse crack and a big pole across my back. SEXY.

In a last bid attempt to be sexy I got a zip round PVC red catsuit.

The zip went from the top of my bum crack all the way round to the to of my cleavage.

It was like the one from the 'oops I did it again' Britney Spears Video.

You could unzip it from ether end!
How hard can it be to make this into a sexy kinky night.

 I had dumped the pole and it was just me and the catsuit.

 What can possibly go wrong !!!

Getting my labia caught in the zip, that's what could and did go wrong.

 I feel sick even now just thinking about it. I actually cried, didn't cry giving birth but this made me whimper like a lost puppy.

I still have a little blood blister to prove it
. I have added zips to the long list of things I'm not safe with!!

A short story about how I fractured my pubic bone by pelvis thrusting a lamp post. Add some vodka and a night out with the girls and that's the story. Both vodka and lampposts are on the list of things I'm not trusted with.

Fanny farts. Only ever did one and it wasn't my fault.

 If you blow up it, it will do it back.
The air can't be absorbed by my womb so it had to come out somewhere!

The fact it was loud and in your face was just funny.
I hope that was a lesson to you all.

Accidentally slipping it up my bum. ….
Definitely not!!
Aim better or I'm shutting shop completely.
I couldn't give a flying badger if you once met someone once ,or read it in a lads mag about how amazing bum play is.
 will tell you now that my bum hole is directly linked to my Gag Reflex and I will karate chop you in the throat if any part of you goes near my rusty sheriff Badge.
I am forever grateful that lee feels the same about his pooper. …..

 Oral sex, if you hear me and Lee saying that we are having sausage and beans For dinner it almost never means actual sausage and beans.
Yes we are childish and no I don't care.

 I do have some advice on oral sex.

If you get a pube in your mouth, style it out with a sexual floss. I'm joking…. How would that even work.

Just remove the pube and flick it on the floor like a normal person.

Spit or swallow, I couldn't care less what other people do.

But did you know there is about 50calories in your average mouthful.
Think about that when you at spinning class.
Where are you even meant to spit it?
That can't be sexy.

How can you tail of a man has a high sperm count??? You have to chew before you swallow …. Sorry I had to slip in a crap joke.

Chapter 6

Rants

This chapter is my favorite and I bet it's the longest.

Being very British I try and keep my controversial options to myself (but lee, he has to listen to my shit, poor bloke).

I don't remember the saying…. Is it options are like arse holes or penises? It's something about it's ok to have one but sometimes it stinks and don't shove it in my face. It might be a saying about religion actually. Ether way you get the point.

Dogs in clothes…… I have 2 dogs. Both own clothes. Leliu (the spitz) came with a bag of clothes ! If ever leliu finds any of her clothes she will try to put them on.

She looks stupid and I'm sure the other dogs must this she is a twat but it causes her no harm. Nancy was given to me as a Pomeranian (Given to me because she has " issues" and the breeder didn't think she would last long),
I know a lot about dog breeds and as an educated guess I think she is a Capuchin Monkey cross with a squirrel.

She walks like your drunk auntie at a wedding reception and we fondly call her the hairy potato.

Nancy has some jumpers, I did buy them for her.
Some were just for taking the odd photo and others are to keep her little tiny body warm in the winter.

Just to explain how small she is, one of the Christmas jumpers she has was sold to fit on a bottle of wine.

Which by the way I think is way more ridiculous than putting a jumper on a dog, what the hell does a bottle of wine need a jumper !

Clothes on dogs…. If it's your dog and they don't mind and it's not hurting them in anyway do what you want.

You are not entitled to an opinion about someone you don't really know (this doesn't included famous people) just because you know someone that used to know that person doesn't give you the right to have an opinion on them.

Especially if it's a negative opinion. Women are the worst for this.

If I haven't personally spent at least 10mins with you one on one ......I do not know you and you do not know me. I also couldn't give a fuck what you think about me.

If I'm having an overly sensitive day I might give a shit and it might even upset me then lee has the job of reminding me that people that don't like me tend to not actually know me. I do make an effort to be a nice person.

One thing everyone seems to have an opinion on, the amount and gender of my children. Yes I know that I have my hands full I know that they are all boys and no I'm not trying for a girl. I don't think I have ever left my house with all of my children with me and somebody not have somebody make a stupid comment or ask a stupid question.

"are they all yours" ?... no love hospital security is really shit and I took them!,, "yes all mine"..... "all boys"???.. last time I checked... "yes they are"... wait for it .... "did you want a girl"???? .... I don't believe you can pick the fucking gender of your children so what a redundant question.... "as long as they were healthy I didn't mind"..... then if they are super brave I get..... " you must get a lot in benefits" ....

I sometimes wish I did you judgmental bitch but I work really hard so my taxes can pay for your dam bus pass.... "no,no i work".... "oh so you are just a part time mother"..... just fuck right off.
 Every single time.

Like I said ,I think you are entitled to an opinion about famous people, especially people that are famous because of reality TV it's kind of your right to have an opinion on them.
Though I have met several famous people and my opinion did change after meeting them face-to-face.
I love all the women on loose women and I think I would be great on that show. Stacy is my idol.

I have an issue with dirty hands, your dirty hands bother me a bit, but my dirty hands drive me to an OCD style boiling water hand scrubbing.
The worst thing is when someone's food gets on your hands when your scraping plates.

If gravy with bits of potato and peas gets on my hands I will flip out.
I always carry had gel and tissues.

Call centres! ....My phone always rings when I'm in the middle of doing something important like making custard.
I always answer like a total rookie.
Then you hear the deafening silence of the 3 seconds it takes for the call to actually connect....
 Normal people have already hung up at this point....
But not me....
"hello is this mrs Marshall" because I can't think quick enough to lie I say ,yes and now I'm talking to someone I can't just hang up.. ....
"my name is John" I am 100% sure that your name is not John....
your accent is so heavy it's barely understandable...,
"I understand you have recently been in a car accident"
I don't like cars John and I haven't been in an accident in the last 5 years
"er no I haven't "....
"has anyone else in your household been in an accident that wasn't their fault"
..... at this point I'm tempted to really fuck johns day up and make up some total shit like....

Well yes my husband was in an accident that killed a young family but he did come away with a burn on his leg from where he dropped his fag, he didn't notice at the time on account of being so drunk,

…."no John , no accidents here"…. "are you sure"…

errrr yes I'm fucking sure… I didn't forget about my broken spine I got in the 17 car pile up you dick..

  at this point I pass the phone to Ethan …. Dude it's John on the phone for you..

"hi john… I'm Ethan. … I just watched the lion King and ate popcorn….

 Mummy .. John is gone" ….BINGO. .

I don't even know what PPI is so I can really rant about that, but I do know a shit tone of people will be looking for a job after the end time to claim is!

Body odour , …...wash your smelly pits.

I don't care if you have to stand outside in the rain rubbing yourself with next doors lavender plant, you make me gag.

There is a man that lives nea

r me that has the worst personal fragrance, every time I go in the local shop I can smell when he is in it too.

He smells like toe jam mixed with fanny on a hot day and old egg.

He has his own brand of B.O, I'm sure it could be bottled and used in a hostage interrogation situation.

Does he not have anyone in his life to buy him soap!

'YES'-people. Don't be a 'yes' person it does not make you a good friend.
I would rather be a " Say Nothing At All person" than a yes person.
When Steve asks if he should go on Britain's Got Talent don't say yes when you know full well that Steve has no fricking Talent.

Say something more productive like ….." seems like a waste of time to me,.....it's a fix".

 Or be brutally honest and say " what fricking Talent will you be attempting to display because it's not obvious to me and I'm pretty sure you will just really embarrass yourself"....

 Or when a girlfriend asks if that dress makes her bum look fat, you know what babe it's not the dress your bum look fat, your fat makes your bum look fat.

So when I asked you what you think of my book Use words like at " least you tried" or " you know some much longer words than I thought you did". But don't tell me you think it's amazing if you have read more interesting cereal packets.

Salt... I do love a a bit of salt on my chips but....when I see TV chefs sprinkling Sea Salt into food, Sea salt is a fantastic natural exfoliator (I have used it many times, as a home made foot scrub). So when the chefs are sprinkling it on the food rubbing their fingers together all I can think of is the dead skin cells from the fingers going in the food. Disgusting. Use a salt grinder or a spoon.

Complaining about food.....it must be a very British thing but why is it whenever we get bad food in a restaurant we complain to the whole table that the food is horrible but when the waitress comes over whilst you have a mouthful of food you nod and gesture that the food is amazing.

Why do we do that. Lee will lean over and tell me that his chicken is burnt one end but raw the other.

Then why the fuck did you just tell the waitress that the food was wonderful?..
why are you telling the whole table that your food is inedible, none of us can do anything about it , the one person that could have helped you in that situation was that waitress that came over and asked you how you're fucking chicken was.

In 10 minutes when she comes to take your plate at with the disgusting chicken on it I'm sure you would tell her to send compliments to the chef. Why do we do that?..

 my mum is excellent at complaining about food, she wins at complaining about food. I
t must be the teacher in her, she gives people that look where they feel bad about themselves. The waitress didn't even cooks the food but you know that she is whole hardly apologising to my mum like it's all her fault and questioning her life choises.

My friend James is also good at complaining but I think he does it to get free stuff more than anything.

 Needless to say they both the great people to take for dinner so they can complain for you.

Cars (selfish drivers too),.... lots of things about cars piss me off.

They stink.

They don't stop at the zebra crossing . yet have the audacity to get pissed at you when you walk over the bonnet in your high heels when they are stopped right in the middle of the crossing!

They are loud at the best of times then boys with little knobs fit a DJ booth on the back parcel shelf and replace the back seats with a speaker.

The car horn should be used to make other road users aware of your presence.
It's not to let your mate kev know that you are outside ready to take him for a drive along felixstowe sea front.

Please don't beep at me if you see me walking down the street, it scares the shit out of me. What do you really expect, should I run along side the car have a chat about the weather through the car window.

No that's not going to happen is it.
I don't know anyone over the age of 20 that hasn't been in a car accident.

Ether you are all shit driving or cars are just dangerous.

It hurts to get hit by a car, this has happened to me 3 times.

One time doesn't count because it was a parked car and I wasn't looking where I was walking. But both other times I was innocent and it hurt!!!

speeding.... don't even get me started on speeding. Why do you need to go that fast, if it says 30 that's for a good reason.

Speeding gets worse as soon as it rains.
You will not get wet, you are in your fucking car.

Your not in a personal booth, your car has window that mean I can see you, I see you picking your nose, I see you texting with your phone in your lap, I see you giving your boyfriend a blowjob. Just stop it.

Snobs.... I don't mind you being a snob and acting like you are better than me if you are actually better than me.

But don't walk around with your nose in the air acting like you don't fart after eating beans.

I'm not sure what things gives you the right to be a snob.
i eat blue cheese and have never owned a chunky gold plated chain, does this make me better than some people?.?..... probably not.
The queen can be a snob... she is definitely better than lots of people.

Rudeness -.. manners cost nothing so give them a bash.

Teach your children to be polite.
Rudeness is just so unnecessary.

Don't be late, your time is not more precious than mine.

Just because someone is being paid to wait on you doesn't give you the right to be rude to them.

Say excuse me.
Hold a door open.

 Move to the side if you see me coming with my buggy.

Don't spit on the floor, its rude and disgusting.
 I don't care if you are old and you think you can make a judgement on me, you can't it's just rude.

If you have nothing nice to say keep your stupid mouth shut.

Whispering is rude too.

Talking with food in your mouth is rude.
Picking your nose in front of me. Use a tissue or something.

Strangers touching my baby.-....
My youngest was born with a full head of hair.
He has had 3 hair cuts already.

You may comment (people always say "he must get all that hair from his dad" what a stupid thing to say! I'm not bald)
 but you don't need to touch it!
 I was in the local shop when a post man (not Chris ,my postman) just a random post man started talking to Alfred and Alfred was giving him his best big smiles...

before I know at was happening the postman took Alfred from his pram and was giving him a hug!, ...

what the actual fuck.

I was trying to do the geometry in my head to work out if I was to kick his legs from underneath him, if I could catch Alfred before he hit the floor.

Lucky for the postman geometry is not a strong point of mine and he had put Alfred back before I could work it out.

I was not impressed.

Old ladies always touch babies with their old arthritic witch fingers and pinch any chubby bits on show.
I might make baby t shirts that say " DONT EVEN THINK ABOUT IT" or a sign to clip on the buggy that says "touch my baby at your own risk, I bite".

I'm not totally happy at people I do know touching my baby, lee is lucky I let him touch Alfred to be honest.

I am a very over protective mother but I have legitimate reasons like..... people have germs and my children are the most precious thing in the universe.

Bluetooth Headsets.-I'm sure that they do have their uses like when you're in a car or something. Walking down the street talking really loudly with this stupid thing hanging off your ear and your phone in your hand just makes you look a total moron.

Hold your phone up to your ear like a normal person.

If you are going to talk that loud you have an obligation to put your phone on speaker phone so I can hear what the other person is saying too!

Topless men/lads.-
I'm not prudish at all and I have no problem seeing nipples.

It really should be in the right context.
 If you are on your property be naked if you like, I might decide to leave if I come over for a cuppa and your husband is walking about with his wanger out.

But it's your home so crack on.
 Once the kids are in bed I like to walk about naked so this isn't a nudity issue.
 I don't care if you are hot, I don't care if you have a 6pack.... keep your top on please.
 Yes of course the beach is fine and in your garden or a swimming pool.

But that's it.

I don't want to see your nipple hair as I'm
getting a coffee from Greg's.

Weed- i've never tried it I don't want to try it last
time I checked it still illegal in this country.
Medicinal marijuana for your glaucoma is
definitely not meant to be smoked in the local
park at 10:40pm so dont give me that shit.
It stinks it stinks like old cat piss, if you smoke it
you smell like old cat piss, your house probably
smells like old cat piss and everything you own
smells like old cat piss.

 In case I haven't made myself really clear I don't
like the smell of old cat piss.

 I make sure that I go out side of my house every
single day, I think it's supposed to be good for
your mental health.

and I honestly can't remember the last day that I
haven't smelled weed.

People walk past me with the kids smoking it.
 I see people during the day dealing it.
I walk past houses with tin foil in the window
obviously growing it.

It boils my piss.

Maybe it's because I've never tried it that I can't understand the appeal.

Everybody that I have ever seen stoned or high never particularly looks that happy.
Maybe they should try taking up a Kinder egg habit.

People always look happy when they have a Kinder Egg.

Mates rates-….
I know lots of my friends will relate to this.
Why do people ask for mate's rates when you are trying to earn a damn living.

I comprehend that I already own the camera I fully understand their I'm invited to the wedding anyway but if you want my expertise as an (award winning) photographer pay for it.

it's not easy and for me to produce over 500 images that i'm happy to put my name on.
it's going to take me a very long time to edit your ugly face and it takes effort.

If Bob down the road can do it for 50 quid go and see Bob down the road.

My wedding packages start at £700.

Somehow in your little brain you think that asking for me to do it as a wedding gift is acceptable.

I was going to stick a £20 John Lewis Gift Card in a card like a normal person.

... So then I would attempt to lie and make out I was already booked for that day or something but anybody that knows me knows that I'm a complete pushover so I would end up doing it and probably pay for a massive canvas print of your favourite photo as well.

We had to deal with this shit when lee published his first book.

Lee bleeding didn't even get a free book so what makes you think that he can get you one.

Spend your £5.99 bring your copy round and I'll get him to sign it for you.

The majority of jobs I have had I have been self-employed whether it be as a make-up artist or a Disney princess I have most definitely missed out on tens of thousands of pounds by doing favours and mate's rates.

So the next time you ask your hairdresser friend who is probably on minimum wage to give you a trim for free think again....

White trousers -
unless you are a girl under the age of 10 ,a
dentist or a celebrity don't even think about it.
 They just look bad and dirty really quickly.
I did get myself (stupidly) some white, ripped
kneed skinny jeans about 4 years ago.

Of course at that's going to be the day that I
spontaneously come on my period 3 days early
and I'm in Woodbridge with the five children.
Never again will I make that mistake.
 When I came home the jeans went in the bin
and I condemned every white pair of trousers to
hell. Don't be a fool like me, pump the brakes
and back the truck up, say no to the white
trousers.

Body shaming-
 This one I feel very passionate about and it's not
spoken about enough.
 I am all for being happy and confident in your
own skin no matter what your size or shape.
I see some of my big beautiful friends posting
pictures of themselves in a two-piece and
everybody taking their hat off to them for
having the confidence to work it,
 and I'm the first person to comment "you go
girl" and promote body confidence.

My issue is when you don't get the same comments if you were a busty size 8 in a thong bikini.

Since when is it ok to call somebody skinny but not somebody fat.
I have been told that I need a cookie (in my slimmer days), but I would be completely wrong to tell an overweight person to step away from the pie.

Body shaming needs to work across the full spectrum.
Being overweight is just as unhealthy as being underweight.
I'm currently still carrying a considerable amount of baby weight, it's hugely affect my confidence but Lee tells me I'm beautiful everyday.
Just be nice and be sensitive to everybody no matter how they look.

Giving credit where It's due-
It really is that simple don't sit there and lap it up when somebody else has done all of the hard work give people credit where credit is due. This advice does not apply to children where you have done their homework for them, let them take the credit.

Yes of course Ethan decorated his Easter hat all by himself, yes it does have moving and light up parts....

yes your child's hat is shit in comparison.
I have arranged many many charity functions and stayed in the Shadows just hoping that somebody would give me a little shout out, but no.
I just sit I
n the corner and listen to all the other thank yous. " a special thank-you to Brenda for her donation of cupcakes, a big thank you to Steve for booking the burger van" so on and so on. Good job I never held my breath waiting for my thanks I would have been dead many times over. And if you think I sound bitter it's because I am.

Eyebrows-
I was a victim of the 90s and over Plucking so have at best 12 hairs left per side.
Annoyingly from those 12 hairs most of them are curly/unruly and I have one grey hair!

I have tried every different make up item known to man for eyebrows.

I even attempted to microblade my own brows (go to a salon like a normal person , dont be a fool like me)
That just gave me brown scabs for 2 weeks so I won't do that again.

I won't leave the house without my eyebrows on as I feel naked and look strange.

I did once go out with just one eyebrow on, I got some looks that day.

On the most part I think I do a good job at doing my eyebrows as most people don't know that they are drawn on.

But my got I have seen some brows in my time...
…..Everyone who got them tattooed in black 10 years ago are regretting it as they are now blue.
Every woman is reading this and nodding in acknowledgment that they know somebody with blue Eyebrows.
We all know the one lady in the office that gave up of the natural look and just has a McDonald's style arch on their   forehead in brown crayon.
Just give them a little shape please sweetheart.
 And what is with these massive daddy caterpillar things that teenagers are rocking these days.

They're supposed to look like eyebrows not like your toupee has slipped.

Unnecessary Noises.--
At number one is whistling, shut up Jeff I don't care if you can do an exact imitation of a bird (so can a bird) or you can whistle a well-known tune, its annoying as fuck.

 I hope you choke on your own spit!

As for wolf whistling.... when's the last time you heard somebody say, me and "Alan have been married for 23 years we first met when he wolf whistled at me.".. never ...you, will never hear that ....,it does not happen.

Loud chewing noises .....that's unnecessary, how can you make a slice of Victoria Sponge sound like you're eating gravel, wet gravel. Meh. It's disgusting. Smacking your lips.... I'm 5 tables away and I can hear you.... I want to drown you in your bowl of tomato soup. Men's snoring is not an unnecessary noise because when they lay down their testicles go over their arsehole and this causes a vapour lock, this is why men should wear tight pants in bed to lift their testicles up. But women snoring is unnecessary.

Snoring when you're awake, is an unnecessary noise. I think it's a dad thing. My dad does it. (I have your back mum).

Clicking fingers, tapping or humming. Pack it in. loud yawning... loud sneezing.. loud hick ups......all can be done in a stifled manner so do it.

People that compare their stuff to my stuff - ...and they don't have a fucking clue what they're talking about .
I know it's apparently all relative but No Karen your broken nail isn't the same as my tumour. What's that you were saying …. You couldn't afford a second holiday this year.
Cry me a fucking river.

I sold my tv so I could do food shopping this week (that's not true but you get me drift). The week after my grandad died I was feeling a bit down as you can imagine and my friend actually said….. "I know how you feel, my hamster died last week"…. Absolutely not!!! Fuck right off.

Moaning about shit that is your fault-...... you are in debt because you buy expensive handbags that you don't need, idiot, stop spending more then is in your bank! Simple.

If you want a decent haircut ,pay for one ,your hair looks shit because you spent £13 on it.
 You are fat because you put more in your mouth thing comes out of your ass, if you are unhappy about it change it don't bitch about it.

Saying that I am a typical woman ,I get upset that i'm fat so I comfort eat and then that makes me more fat.

I try not to complain about my lack of sleep, I chose to have a baby, (I did not choose for him to still require feeding every 2 hours at 4 months old but shit happens).

 If you moan that your tired because you went to see Ed Sheeran live in concert I will kick you in the lungs.

Do not drink your entire body weight in lager and then complain that you a have a hangover the next day.

If you have unprotected sex you deserve gonorrhoea!

Hypochondriacs and people that think they are doctors-.

One of my friends who is a hypochondriac and has something wrong with her every time I have ever seen her , I managed to convince that she probably needed to get her prostate checked!

Watching 2 hypochondriacs in a conversation is quite entertaining, how they somehow try and outdo each other with their ailments.
These are the sorts of competitions that surely nobody wants the win, I don't care whose incontinence is worse than the others.
 Is your arm fractured, is it sprained, does it even have a bruise..... no ,well no you didn't almost break it and you definitely don't need a sling.

Just because you have had most illnesses and injuries known to man doesn't make you a Dr. Just because your husband is a Dr doesn't make you a Dr. You might work at a Drs surgery but unless you work their as a Dr you are not a Dr.

I don't like horses-
 yet my favourite animal is a unicorn.
I have never been bit by unicorn but I have been bit by every horse that I have ever come close enough to.

I managed to go to Ladies Day at the Races and not even see a horse.

I appreciate that they are beautiful , wise animals.
But I'm quite convinced that they are only opposable thumbs away from taking over the universe.
I don't understand why you would want to ride one or have one as a pet.
They smell bad and they really dusty.
I would be interested in having a miniature donkey as a pet.
I would want to keep one in those plastic playhouses meant for children.
I would call him Stephen and bring him in from the garden when people were around for a cuppa it seems like he would make a good talking piece.

Self service checkouts-
If I wanted to work in pound land I would apply. The stupid thing shouts at me every time…. "My item is in the fucking bagging area"….
Then sally comes along rolling her eyes at you, she jiggles some of you're shopping then swipes her magic card and you can continue doing her job again.
This happens at least 5 times and I only have fucking items 7 items.

I'm sure sally doesn't even actually even check if I'm trying to rob myself a bottle of shampoo and she probably doesnt care and you know what I don't blame her.

On line shopping substitutions-…. i'm eternally grateful for the fact that I never have to leave my house if I don't want to, I can have literally everything sent to me by shopping on line.
 Not having to take the kids shopping with me to buy food is a total god send.

But when you're trying to be vegan for a month and instead of the soya milk you ordered you get sent full fat Jersey cow milk That's going to fuck things up.

Some substitutes are fine, chopped tomatoes are chopped tomatoes but tampons and size5 nappies are not the same thing even in an emergency and your feeling inventive.

  my porridge would not taste good if I used the coriander instead of the cinnamon I actually ordered.

Sometimes it's funny and me and Steve the driver have a giggle but Riley wasn't happy that he was sent a fifi the flower tots birthday cake instead of Spider-Man!

The weather.-
I'm not good with weather .
If it's hot my eyebrows melt off my face and I am a sweaty mess...

my head sweats more than any other body part, I look like I have just walked out the shower with my wet hair sticking to my face like seaweed to a rock.

If it's cold I get freezing, I have special thermal gloves, socks and vest.

Most normal people would be able to go on an artic mission in comfort but not me.

My finger and toes go blue with blotches of white and orange, my nipples get so hard and erect they could cut glass.

The only time I don't feel the cold is when I'm pregnant but it's a bit much to be pregnant every winter.

Watching lee jump out the bed when I put my cold feet on his leg is one plus point.

You can time the rain with school runs.

Every dam time I leave the house with the buggy (so you can't hold an umbrella) to get the boys from school it chucks it down, then it stops the second the kids come out and they look at you like you're a soaking wet embarrassment on purpose.

I do love clouds, I like cloud watching.

You can always find a rabbit and a whale in the clouds.

Thunder storms are great to watch and make for amazing photos if you have a good camera.

The thing I hate most in the whole world has to be bullying-

I hate that all of my (school age) children have experienced bullying.
I did tell an 8 year -old boy that I would poo in his lunchbox if you didn't leave my son alone!
I figured if I threaten to punch him in the face I would get in trouble, no adult he's going to believe another adult had threatened to poo in a Childs lunchbox.

It's definitely not something I would advise doing you really shouldn't tell children you were going to poo in their lunchbox but for me it worked so I don't have any real regrets.
 It's disgusting that I have seen bullying in the workplace and amongst friends.

I think the worst bullying I have seen is amongst mums , specifically playground Mums, every woman who has ever done a school run and knows exactly what I am talking about.
Just because that you are an adult does not mean that you are exempt from being a bully.
  If you don't like somebody that's fair enough you don't have to like everybody, but keep your biased unjustified opinions to yourself.

And just as a warning if you decide to bully any of my mummy friends I will threaten to poo in your lunchbox!

Chapter7

LGBTQ+

I didn't know if I should do this chapter or not, I decided to keep it in and keep it short.
It was a really difficult time in my life but by chance ended up working part time in a gay pub (the arb), i can't imagine where I would be now if I hadn't.

Love is love, as long as it's legal I couldn't care less what gender you are attracted to and I don't care what's between your legs as it's not any of my business.

I was on a night out for Jo's birthday and we ended up in the arb for some karaoke with mark. James and kaka were working behind the bar and the pub was packed.
I have an anxiety disorder so being in a busy bar of people I don't know would normally send me into a panic.
This group of the most visually exciting people I have ever seen are also the most open and honest people I have ever met.

I left that night with a job and 17 friends for life that happen to be part of my local LGBTQ+ Community.

I have learnt lots of things from my Arb friends that would have been a questionable google search.

I know what a gold star and a platinum gay is, I know what a spaghetti lesbian is and I know the difference between a top and a bottom gay!!!
I'm not going to say what they all are because I like the idea of some of my more prudish friends now texting to ask me he he.

I have been to many burlesque Shows ran by the cheeky devils club that have left me baffled, amazed and sometimes sexually confused.
What a group of talented people. I take my hat off to you all.
What a skill and confidence I could only dream off.
I have to also add that it was a lot less nudity than I imagined it would be and a lot more emotive!
I love that everyone I have made friends with from the arb has a story to tell, I would buy all of your books.
Everyone had come through so much.

I had an eye-opening conversation with one of the more mature transgender ladies, she was a child in the early 60s when she tried to explain to her parents that she was trapped in the wrong body.

Her parents took her to the family GP and explained that their son was very confuse and thought that he was a girl.

So this young boy who felt trapped in the wrong body was given electric shock therapy testosterone injections and antidepressants to make him happy about being male.!!!!

This of course didn't work because she was a female trapped in the males body.

She now seems like a very content transgender woman and A lot better looking than most women I know of her age and younger.

I took my wonderful transgender friend Jen for her first bra fitting.

The ladies at Debenhams treated us completely normally as they should.

I was chuffed that Jen let me be a part of that day. I feel like I made help make a life time memory.

There is still so much ignorance in the world, although we have obviously come along way from electric shock therapy and at last same-sex marriage is legal.

But I have witnessed hate towards some of my friends just because of their sexual orientation or they way they dress or what they may or may not have between their legs.

don't get me wrong I have on occasion got my pronouns wrong but that's because I'm a bit slow not because I'm trying to be rude or hateful.

My ex actually once said just because you're dressed like Scooby Doo doesn't mean I'm going to pretend you're a dog!!!

You know what sweetheart I expect you to spend your life in bliss with that level of ignorance.

I would rather be somebody's tequila slammer than everybody's cup of Tea!!! Let's take it up the arb (do you remember the t.shirts I had made?)!!!

Me and lee had our first kiss outside the arb coming to think of it and James is the fairy godfather of our son.

If you are ever in Ipswich go and get a tattoo or piercing get it done from one of the guys at twisted monkey (tell them I said hi) or see if your lucky enough to catch a show put on my the cheeky devil club.

The arb is now a restaurant, a very lovely restaurant but it's not our pub anymore.

I have the upmost love and admiration for every single one of you , you know who you all are. I owe more to you than most of you will ever realise.

Chapter 8

Education

My qualifications … I have loads of qualifications. I think I was trying to prove a point.

I have 11 GCSEs, 10 of them are A-C but I got a D in math.

Rightly so I am shit at maths.

From school I went to college to do an NVQ2 in beauty therapy.

It was a shit load more written work than expected but it was fun.

I then did a few weekend training courses In special effects make -up and aromatherapy massage.

I tried to set up my first business called lilies lovelies using my beauty skills.

It didn't last long. …..

. started a job working for care UK so did my carer with the Elderly qualifications.

I worked with some deaf people so decided to go back to college to learn BSL.

I did my level 2.

I can't remember much of it now but I was able to teach the boys a bit.

I had worked with a few photographers as their make up artist and was made to feel like I was too stupid to use their expensive cameras even though I enjoyed taking photos as A hobby.

So like the petulant child that I am I enrolled myself in night college and studied photography for Year (got a b-tec).

I ended up winning an award for the V&A and having my work displayed in the Morley the gallery in London. In your face sexist pigs.

I then got offered a place at the University but family life came first and I turned it down.

Two years ago I got an array of diplomas and managed to get distinction in them all.
So on my wall in loo you will see the following framed certificates.
Parapsychology, Child psychology, Family and relationship counseling (shock myself with that one), cognitive behavioral therapist, hypnotherapy practitioner , postnatal depression awareness and neurolinguistic programming.
Not bad hey.
What dyslexia means to me…. I don't actually know whereabouts on the dyslexic Spectrum my am but I am highly functioning I think.
My reading and writing is probably the same level of the average eight-year-old.
I can guarantee that you would be able to write quicker than I could read.
But I am very artistic and more determined than most.
It took me a long time to come to terms with the fact that I have dyslexia and that my abilities to learn some things might not be the same as everyone else. I
remember blowing out my candles on my birthday cake when I was 10 and making my wish to not be dyslexic anymore.

If I'm completely honest I wouldn't be dyslexic if I could choose but I'm definitely not going to let it hold me back.

It doesn't define me as a person. It doesn't make me stupid.

Heck I'm writing a book!!!

A story about my dyslexia which will make my dad laugh.

When I had to have several different types of IQ test my dad came with me.

One of the tests they bought through a large tray with different items and it was left with me in a room with it for about 15 minutes, the lady came back in the room took the tray away,.

The lady asked me what I remembered from the items on the tray.

I asked her what tray???

Facepalm moment for my dad.

I honestly don't know where my brain was that day.

What qualifications I still want- midwifery has interested me since having my Children.

If you ask Lee he will tell you that he is basically already a midwife because he delivered our son (True story).

My response is that I once tie-dyed T-shirt and it doesn't make me a fashion designer!!!

Maybe I will look into nursing again now that is my fear of people dying and blood is almost gone.

Being a psychologist in a mental health unit intrigues me and I think I would be quite good at it so that's a avenue to look at.

I absolutely love learning and the world is my oyster so I'm sure I will pick up some more qualifications and to fill the rest of my wall in the toilet.

You learn a lot from different jobs that you have So I tell you about some of the jobs that you've had and you can guess the sort of things I might have learnt from them. I've worked in bars and restaurants, as a beauty therapist , make up artist and massage therapist, carer, Anne Summers representative, adult party planner, Feminising contouring make up classes for transgenders, baby sign language teacher, photographer, Artist, advertising , promotion, counsellor, hypnotherapy practitioner , Youth support worker, dog breeder, online shop owner, Fashion blogging, double glazing sales rep, Multilevel marketing , paranormal investigator and probably some other stuff I can't remember. So the array off different skills I have picked up along the way is massive.

As well as the wonderful things that my children learn at school I hope that I can pass on some pearls of wisdom and educate them in some of the practical ways I feel I missed out on when I was at school.

I might be wrong but I feel sure that children are still leaving school without the ability to iron a shirt or have a clue about mortgage rates.
This stuff is important.
Maybe schools should give out a leaflet to parents to let us know what they are doing and what bit we are supposed to do. I don't want to stand on anyone's toes I will most definitely be leaving Pythagoras and chemistry to you.
But if you could fit in comparable rates and how to make a decent casserole that would be great. I seem to be "helping" my kids with homework that's definitely school stuff not mummy stuff.

I absolutely love school, it's just such a shame that I hated the lessons but the social part of school was great.
I didn't hate all lessons, Just the ones that you had to read and write in.
drama, music, dance, art, food tech…. I liked that bit. Education as it is the moment isn't that well adapted for kinaesthetic learners like myself and exams are definitely not made for learners like myself with anxiety. But until I am prime minister or queen of the world I don't think it's going to change.

Chapter 9

Relationships

my first boyfriend was probably Thomas, well
he was a boy and he was my friend.
If t wo-year-olds can I have a boyfriend then he
was that.
I definitely kissed him.
From the age of 6 to about the age of 10 boys
were disgusting.
I don't know why anybody would even want to
talk to a boy let alone Anything else.
From the age of 10 to maybe 11 boys were good
for practicing getting married to.
The fake wedding's where a good way to spend
your lunchtime at primary school.
We did play kiss chase quite a lot but I think it
was more exciting having the boys running
away from you screaming that was fun rather
then actually getting to kiss them if you manage
to catch up with one of them.

Then you go to high school, I had to up my
game pretty quick.
I'm sure some of the kids were losing their
virginity at about the age of 12 ,or at least saying
they did.

at the age of 12 I was still getting my head around the idea that somebody might put their tongue in my mouth let alone their penis in my Vagina.

I had the two terrifying erection / pen incidences. I ended up marrying the first person that I had a real relationship with, I wouldn't advise anybody else do that FYI.

The first date I ever went on I didn't know it was a date until the next!

I have never really been on a date before meeting my first husband and I didn't really go on a date with my first husband ever. .

A little while after me and Gary split up one of my male friends (for all intents and purposes we should call him Chris) asked me if I wanted to go out for dinner to cheer me up.

Sounded legitimate he was my friend, I was upset he wanted to cheer me up.

He came to my home address to pick me up with a bunch of Flowers , that was nice of him!

We went out for Curry and to the cinema.

I think we saw one of the mummy films it was so long ago I don't actually remember that bit.

Then after the film he asked if I wanted to go back to his and watch a bit of TV.

Sure thing why not sounds better than going back to my empty house .

We went up to his bedroom laid on the bed and watched several episodes of "friends" who doesn't love a bit of "friends".

It got to about 2 am so I asked if he could give me a lift home!

He asked if he could walk me to my front door I thought that was a bit weird seeing as it was about four steps from the door of the car, so I said no but thanks for a smashing night catch you later.

With a belly full of curry I took myself up to bed and fell asleep as soon as my head hit the pillow.

I woke up to several messages on my phone from Chris trying to work out what he done wrong and why I didn't seem to appreciate the date.

Total face-palm moment. ,,,,,Oh it was a date …..
I didn't see Chris again after that.

I did also have another friend try and kiss me ,I must of given him the totally wrong impression because I had no interest in him and never have., had.

The most embarrassing part of that story is I went to text my friend to tell her that he had tried to kiss me and it was disgusting and so on and So on…

and accidentally sent the text to him.

Why does this stuff always me!!!

He's not my friend anymore either.

I've had my fair share of bad relationships but I don't think this is the book to go into it.

Let's talk about the good parts of a relationship, they should be fun they should make you smile and laugh.

I love going on adventures, this means we put our walking shoes on and keep walking until we can't walk anymore.

I one time found what I was very convinced was a unicorn.

It took my breath away in the middle of nowhere on a beautiful patch of green on a late spring morning,

it was there almost shimmering in the light break between the trees.

I said lee look , look over there I see a unicorn.

He said baby I don't mean to shatter any illusions but that is just a white horse .

I told him that he was being mean and I was sure it was a unicorn. I

 did the only test I know how.

To this day I have always been bit by any horse I have gone near enough for it to bite me.

That I have never been bit by a unicorn.

So I approached the mystical beast.

Held out my hand.

And it bit me.

The bastard bit me hard.

Almost took my arm off. (slight exaggeration)...

So it was definitely a horse.

A note to myself and to everyone reading this ...do not approach animals even if there isn't a sign telling you not to you.... really shouldn't. (I have a photo of me approaching the horse just before the attack)

On another one of our adventures we decided to go foraging, we had clearly been watching way too much naked in afraid at the time.

I ate some questionable berries against Lee's recommendations, came out in a rash, was violently ill.

Then did basically exactly the same thing two weeks later because I'm not one to learn from my mistakes.

We have a beautiful fire pit in the garden they're apparently can also be used as a Barbecue.

It takes about 17 bags of coal on account of its large size.

I only had two bags of coal and was determined to cook a sausage yes A single sausage.

I know my boundaries.

I don't know how the hell it did but it did take four hours to cook my singular sausage and the coal was getting cold by the time the sausage was just beginning to get going so we used other fuel sources .

We managed to set fire to a whole bag of hot-dog rolls and three large family sharing packets of flaming hot Doritos which was ironic because once on the fire pit they definitely were flaming hot.

Nobody ate the sausage I think that's a good thing but it was definitely cooked,... mission completed.

Do you ever laugh so hard that you're almost sick and you can't breathe and you have tears rolling down your face.
 This is a weekly occurrence in mine and Lee's relationship.
I have tried nearly every day for the last four years to make Lee jump, I haven't done it yet but I will keep trying.
The thing is every time I hide the anticipation that he might jump I find so funny I'm giggling to myself so it ruins the element of surprise.
This normally just results in Lee sticking his head under the bed going " get out you idiot".

We continuously insist on shoving food in each other's faces and have gone through several cans of canned cream just squirting it at each other.

We have exactly the same childish sense of humor. I can't express enough how important the humor is.
Romance is very important I am ridiculously romantic and Lee even gives me a run for my money.
 We leave each other notes everywhere, he writes in the condensation on the mirror when I'm in the shower.

I drew him little pictures of Wales and bunnies and hearts and leave them where I know he'll find them , for example tucked in his favourite mug.

If I make him a fry-up I will write in ketchup and brown sauce round the edge of the plate.

Lee would hide love letters in my suitcase when I was going away for work.

I personally hate the gift of cut flowers.

I buy them for other people though but please don't buy them for me.

They smell funky after a week.

I don't have a vase.

I get a bit sad when they die and I would rather you got me some shoes!

The saying is… flowers say I'm sorry and chocolates say I love you.

I have lost count of how many times me and Lee have proposed to each other.

Lee insists I was the first one to ask him ,I insist that was not a proposal.

I asked him if he would marry (As in hypothetically one-day would he) he said yes and then insisted that that meant we were going to get married.

The next day he even got a bag of jelly rings and wore a jelly ring around the house singing "I'm getting married in the morning".

He Even flashed his jelly ring at the woman in the co-op saying do you like my beautiful ring I'm getting married don't you know.
She gave him a strange look for obvious reason.
My favourite time that lady proposed to me was probably when he put an engagement ring on one of our kittens legs and told me I could keep the kitten but only if I married him.
It was more romantic than it sounded and definitely better than the time he proposed to me in our favorite restaurant and just said don't be a bitch ...you marry me!
My original engagement ring was a vintage gold ring with three opals in it ,which is my favorite stone and my birth stone.
Unfortunately at the center stone fell out when I was in my parents swimming pool never to be found again.
I was devastated but Lee found this a good excuse to buy a series of costume jewellery rings and propose to me in lots of different ways with them .
He has them put inside the center of a bath bomb .
Hidden in a happy meal toy,.
floating in a helium balloon,.
in a glass of champagne,.
In the middle of a field along with a treasure map (I still don't know how he pulled that one off).

I can't even remember some of the other ways
and he will tell me off for that but I know for
sure this man love me more than anything in the
world.
And before you ask again Lee the answer is yes.

Why I call lee my whale –
before me and lee got together we were mates,
we instantly clicked.
Lee would sometimes come and prop up the bar
if it was quiet and we would put the world to
rights.

One night lee came in and could tell from my
face I was having a bad day.
In his attempt to make me smile he decided to
make random animal noises at me every time I
went to his end of the bar.
Lee is terrible at animal noises but he got me to
crack a smile with his whale impressions.
The splosh noise at the end really did it for me.
From that moment on if ever I was upset or
unhappy in any way Lee would always do the
whale to crack a smile.
This is why I tattooed a while on the bottom of
my foot so I always had a whale on my soul .
But I did wear away to almost nothing so I need
to put another one.
Lee used to phone me when I was at work just to
make whale noises down the phone.

Making whale noises when I was giving birth
even worked to make me smile.

The reason Lee calls me bunny -
is a much shorter story, I twitch my nose when
I'm sleepy, so he called me sleepy bunny that got
shortens too bunny.
I have tattooed a bunny on the top of Leeds foot
and he calls it his lucky rabbits foot!!

I learnt the hard way but there is a very
important lesson in love.
Everyone has a very specific way that they need
to be loved.
Some people need to be showered in expensive
gifts to feel loved.
Some people just need to be told it every now
and again.
Some people love is very physical.
There are loads of different ways to be loved.
It's taking time to work out how the person you
love needs to be shown it.
We often make the mistake of loving somebody
the way that we want to be loved and not the
way that they need it.
And you're not going to just learn it overnight
and communication is definitely the key.
It takes some fine tuning but once it's right it's
right.

Our handfasting ceremony-
it was so very 'us' and perfect in every way. It was small and intimate and we only invited the people that we wanted to not people that we thought we had to and people only came that wanted to and not thought that they had to. My dress was £18 from Amazon and like a long Marilyn Monroe style dress, I had fake flowers in my hair and very simple make up.
Lee looked incredibly handsome in his grey suit with dusky pink tie.
We spent about a month decorating birdcages and glass tea light holders.
We set up an outdoor photo booth with props and a Polaroid camera,.
The idea was that people could take selfies with the Polaroid camera and stick them in the guestbook (We had 3 bum photos put under our pillow).
I managed to find a Victorian poetry book of love poems in lee's favourite bookshop in Felixstowe.
I got a heart shaped hole punch and used it to make confetti.
 I got wildflower seeds and put them in little glass bottles for wedding favours with a little tag on each bottle that said watch our love grow.
 Traditionally pagan handfasting is are held from dusk until dawn. We did this bit.

As our guests entered the beautifully decorated garden they were passed a Tealight.

Mine and Lee's rings were passed around the guests so they could be warmed in filled with well wishes.

At 8:37 which was dusk, I walked down the garden that was lit by candle lights.

Lee took my hand and mouthed that I looked stunning, he had a tear in his eye.

Dom performed the ceremony.

We had written our own vows and made sincere promises to each other.

 After our first kiss as husband and wife I gave Lee his first marital duty and asked him to help take my shoes off for me as I was sinking in the grass.

That's one of my favourite photos of the two of us.

We all celebrated through till dawn.

We mainly don't drink these days so had fruit punch ,With edible glitter and floating lights in it.

We're not massive fans of cake either so our wedding cake was made up of nine different wheels of cheese.

Three different types of marshmallows were available for melting on the open fire.

We got the special sachets that you put on the fire and they made the flames change colour.

 It was magical.

Nemo took some lovely photos for us.

Lee had made futon type beds are out of old wooden crates to line both sides of the garden, my obsession with the bedding and blankets came in handy.

Jenna did the music and I had my wonderful bridesmaids helping look after the boys and melting marshmallows for them.

Our guess had gone by about 3 o'clock in the morning and me and Lee stayed up to watch the sunrise. I

did fall asleep for a little bit in Lee's arms and woke up looking like a unicorn as I had a massive bug bite right in the middle of my forehead.

It was all just perfect, people still talk about it now (3 years on).

I then changed my name legally on our 1year anniversary (it's paper).

Just waiting for the right time to do the boring paperwork wedding. Maybe another baby first....

Ethan currently has 20 girlfriends I don't know that they all know that they are his girlfriends but this is what he tells me.

Brody has one girlfriend at the moment called Olivia, Brody says that she is his girlfriend because she gave him a Valentine's Day card back in February 8 months ago …..seems fair enough.

Riley is 10 so he is going for the stage where the girls are pretty disgusting and he has absolutely no need for any sort of girlfriend in his life.

Harrison has been with his girlfriend for about six months Maybe even longer ,I am sure he will correct me when I ask him later ,but he is so super loved up with her . It is so sweet ,he is saving up to buy her a birthday present next month and he knows exactly what he wants to get.

Josh is had a couple of semi serious relationships but he is almost 18 so I didn't ask what his relationship status is at the moment and I don't think I really want to know as long as I'm not going to be a grandmother any time soon.

Of course we sometimes have arguments, every healthy relationship has arguments if you don't argue it means you haven't got any passion left and your relationship isn't worth why is it fighting for.

I have found that the best way to defuse any argument is to get one breast out.
Lee finds it really hard to stay mad at me if I am exposing myself.

Or if we are in a public place he will stop an argument just to stop me from exposing myself. Seeing as I'm a qualified relationship counsellor I should probably have thought of a better method but this one works fine.

Don't go to sleep on an argument or if you me you won't sleep anyway.
I always have the last word so if I have said my bit and Lee opens his mouth is the start of a new argument.
My favourite arguments we have ever had......
was when we were picking a name for the goldfish (this goldfish we took home in a plastic cup from Charlotte's party, I had to stop Lee from drinking the water because he was on autopilot having a cup in his hand he kept wanting to drink from it) soooooo I wanted to call it Olaf and lee wanted to call it Dr bubbles. After a good 2hrs of fighting our corners we decided to do 'Rock Paper Scissors' to decide the winner.

but lee keep making up his own moves in the game he re names ' Rock paper scissors and anything else he wants' needless to say atomic bomb beat Unicorn so lee won.
This was also the only argument that I let lee win.
Hence why the cat is called Barry. Crab....

Ex is an ex for a reason. I hate it when people say "you loved them once" and stupid things like that.

Of course you love them that's why you put up with them for as long as you did but obviously there was a reason why you split up,

so that's also going to be a reason why you don't wanna be friends with them and don't love them anymore.

I am grown so I can be civil but I don't have to be your friend.

Im not getting you a Christmas card and I would rather that my friends and family didn't get you one ether …..

Chapter 10

Kids/parenthood

Prepare yourselves for a long chapter.
I'm going to start with some of the funny things
that happened during my pregnancies.......
 Had to go to one of my scans with a somewhat
embarrassing burn right across my stomach ,
I was ironing my top wearing just my bra ready
to go to the scan and caught the edge of the iron
across my bump, it hurt like fuck but apparently
happens all the time. I
'm sure that's just something the sonographer
told me to make me feel a bit better about my
stupidity.

I was sick on Lee,.... he gagged on a straw it
made me laugh so hard that I farted which made
me laugh even harder till I was sick on Lee's leg.

Kat had really bad sickness and was once sick in her daughters lunchbox while standing in the playground, it wouldn't of been so bad but it was the morning drop-off not pick up. So it was full.

Some bloke was staring at my massive pregnant breasts whilst I was walking around the shops and when he got level to me I got a waft of his very strong cheap aftershave and dry heaved in his face!!! A big embarrassing moment but it proved a point.

Pregnancy gas is a real thing,..... I don't think Lee had even heard me fart until I was pregnant (maybe once in my sleep).

Then it was like I had a little man playing the bugle behind me every time I walked, bent over or laughed. I

 found it funny most of the time but sometimes was mortified.

 Do you know those plastic chairs that they have in schools that you have to sit on when you attend parents evening they make your farts sound really loud, Yep that was embarrassing. Even more embarrassing when you tried to pass it off as the child that farted and the teacher looks at you and says it wasn't him was it.

No it wasn't teacher but can we all just play along. I

decided to wax my intimate areas whilst pregnant, I use hot wax which means I had to use talcum powder in that area.

If you accidentally get talcum powder on your bum and then fart as you pull off a strip of wax whilst kneeling in front of a mirror in living room it creates amusing fat clouds..... Well Lee found it very amusing, was utterly disgusted with myself.

Farting at funerals is not socially acceptable, but sometimes unavoidable.

I have been incredibly fortunate to not suffer with any form of pregnancy or postpartum incontinence.

But I have no problem telling you some embarrassing stories that happened to some of my friends.

Hellen couldn't go over a speed bump without peeing a bit, this was particularly amusing because as the road she lived on does have lots of speed bumps.

I found this out when going with her to toys 'r' us, ...there are lots of small spiky speed bumps in the car park.

Her face was a picture., with every bump. I found it funny.... she did not.

My friend Jo popped round to use my toilet before going into town, she tripped coming into my house on the step and pissed herself on the hallway floor, she wasn't hurt so I was allowed to laugh.

it wasn't due to bladder weakness but I did wet my knickers once when I was pregnant,....
I often don't wear underwear, not because I'm kinky more because I am lazy.
When you're heavily pregnant you can't look down and see if you're wearing underwear or not because the bump is in the way.
I needed the toilet I went into the rest room pulled my trousers down and sat down on the loo went for a wee and only then realised I was wearing underwear that day.
It wouldn't of been so bad had I of not been in a restaurants rest room.
I had to put my knickers in the sanitary bin.
I was in there for so long everyone must've thought I was doing a big poo. (it didn't help Lee saying loudly... did you have a good poo babe)

I was admitted to hospital for the last week of my pregnancy with Alfred.

I was bleeding and terrified , about five minutes after I got onto the ward (Before I was checked over ,so was scared and worried) The catering lady came round to see if I wanted any lunch that was being Served shortly.

she handed me a tablet and asked me to look through and click on what I wanted.

I must add that lee was with me but had gone to the loo.

The catering lady said "Oh you have chosen the vegan bean casserole …. I will have to see if we have any vegan yogurt for your pudding or would a banana be ok" still not very 'with it' I just said "yeah, thanx".

I had all my checks by the dr and midwife, baby was fine but it was decided that I had to spend the reminding week of my pregnancy in hospital until I was induced.

Not the most convenient thing but needs must as long as the baby was okay I was okay.

A little while later lunchtime came and Lee had popped home to get me a bag of things.

The catering lady gave me my tray of vegan bean casserole ,a soya yoghurt and a banana.

(I had been vegetarian in my younger years, but I have been for the majority of my adult life a non-vegan meat eater all be it picky).

I ate my lunch like a good girl, it was ok as far as beans go.

After the catering lady had cleaned away my tray she came and sat on the end of my bed. Catching me slightly off guard she began a conversation about veganism..,, I made agreeing noises in the right places but wasn't really listening…, then she asked "How long have you been vegan??" …… I'm not vegan…. I just clicked on anything …… I'm just being polite .. did I say any of this.,, no I didn't …. I said "15 years". ….

Why the fuck did I say that….

What a stupid lie…

catering lady seemed very impressed at my 15 year achievements and complimented me on my lifestyle choices.

I didn't think much more of it.

Lee came back with my bags. … The nice catering lady came round with the tea and coffee trolley…. I asked for a coffee , white with one and lee requested the same.

Catering lady politely asked Lee if he too would be having soya milk in his Coffee… lee looked confused and said no thank you.

Catering lady threw him an evil look and almost slammed his coffee (with cows milk) down in front of him.

She sweetly smiled at me and handed me my vegan coffee…. I shook my head at lee and pretended to be disappointed in him.

Catering lady pushed her trolley out of the bay... lee looked at me... I shrugged my shoulders.... "what the fuck was that about, why does that lady hate me"...

"because you're not supporting me being a vegan"....

"but you're not vegan so why would I "....

"because she thinks I'm vegan"... "why would she think your vegan ???" ....

"well I told her I was vegan for 15 years"....

. "I was gone for 2hrs and now you're a vegan" ... "

I didn't mean to"...

"what are you like"...

well lee that was just the tip of the iceberg.

The nice lady ordered me vegan food for the rest of my stay in hospital.

My helpful dad sent me photos of sausage sandwiches and roast dinners!!!

Good son of mine Harry snuck me in milk chocolate and lee pretended it was his.

Friday came and I was looking forward to some different staff over the weekend so I could eat non-Vegan food.

Friday evening catering lady came to wish me the best for my induction on the Sunday.

She then reassured me that she had left a note for the weekend staff to tell them that I was vegan!!! Fuck.

This was not the only example of me being overly and unnecessarily polite.

Somewhere in my head I feel like I will be putting somebody out if I say yes to something they are offering.

This has been proved with the lack of pain relief I have had both during and after giving birth.

When I was asked if I would like to try some gas and air I said "no thank you" I meant to say "I want an epidural Please".

6 children no pain relief…. I'm not brave …. I am stupid.

With Riley it wasn't even any time to offer me anything (3mins) but I'm sure I would of had something with the others.

With Alfred I did hypnobirthing it sounds like hippy shit but it does work.

40min labour ,only 5mins I would say really hurt and lee got to deliver him.

The most amazing moment of both of our lives undoubtedly.

Every pregnancy I have said to myself to eat really healthily so the baby will come out only ever wanting to eat healthy food and I won't be the size of a house.

Unfortunately pregnancy cravings did not allow this to happen.

With josh I craved wham bars, Harry was curry, Riley was paper (specifically toilet roll), Brody was apple juice , Ethan was cheese with green apples, Alfred was beef.

Why is it never celery.

The last trimester Should just be known as the one where you're really hungry , tired and grumpy! , so I just ate rubbish all day .

When josh was weighed and they said he was 6 lb 15 oz I remember thinking surely he must be at least six stone.

But no I really was just massive.

All the boys are good eaters so it didn't have a negative affect thank goodness.

You have to give up loads off good stuff when you're pregnant , you can't eat pate you can't drink vodka for breakfast (you shouldnt do that anyway) you can't smoke cigars, you can't even pickup cat poo!!

Ok some things you can't do are a good thing. When Riley was in special care I got my mum to bring me a wheel of blue cheese with a spoon, that was the best cheese I ever had.

I had 4D scans with all of the boys other than Josh because they weren't invented then, I did of course find it amazing seeing my beautiful babies in 4D.

It's not appreciated when people tell you that the pictures look like aliens or scary or Michelin man Or caspa the friendly ghost.!!!
However true that maybe , expectant parents do not want to hear it ,So lie.

Here is a list of things to not say to the pregnant woman unless you want to be punched in the throat-
Are you sure there's only one in there?

You look like you're much further along.

I bet you're disappointed The gender.

You don't actually have to eat for two you know.

You look shattered.

You should call your baby this…..(insert family name)
…..,,……. 'Insert any advice that has not been asked for'!

Your vagina is going to end up looking like a punched lasagna!

When are you having your next one / are you going to stop now?

Was it planned?

Please just think before you speak.

This might just be me but when I'm pregnant
and somebody insists on buying me or the baby
a gift ....for example at your baby shower I
don't actually want anything for the baby,.
I want to pick all the stuff for the baby myself.
But I think that I could always do with some nice
expensive bubble bath or a pregnancy massage
or vouchers to get my nails done or something
for me. Just saying.

After I give birth I am more than happy to have
you round just so I can show my baby off to you
.
this doesn't necessarily mean I want you to
touch the baby !
you may see him from a distance and make me a
coffee and bring me cake!
when the baby is roughly 6 months old then you
may touch him you have washed your hands.
No I'm not being over the top just my children
are my universe.
Babies are only babies for such a short period of
time and there is not enough hours in the day to
snuggle them and kiss them and cuddle them so
I'm not sharing that time with anybody other
than maybe Lee, our mums.

Dannie and Kat count yourself lucky that you are exceptions to that and thank you for abiding by to my very strict rules on how to touch my baby and the no kissing rules.

Mum guilt- this comes in so many forms. It starts from even before you get pregnant. Am I too young , am I too old , have I got enough money, is my relationship is stable enough, do I already have too many children (that one should of crossed my mind but doesn't).

Then when you're pregnant....did I remember to take the right vitamins, I accidentally fell asleep on my back, I forgot to attend a midwife appointment, I didn't sing to my bump every day.

Then you have labour and delivery guilt....if you used any sort of pain relief that comes with guilt (although I find that funny, because if you have a headache people find it natural to take a painkiller, yet if you're having a tiny human coming out of your vagina it's classed as failing if you opt for an epidural), having to decide whether you want the baby to be delivered straight on to your skin blood and sticky stuff and all or whether you want baby cleaned up and close to before you have your first snuggles are decisions that have to be made which will probably be fulled with guilt (I personally want all the messy stuff and I have cut 3 cords).

Breastfeeding ,bottle feeding, combine feeding …. Cosleeping …independent sleeping…. Going to toddler groups

Swimming classes ,massage classes baby sign language classes….

went to go back to work or if you're going back to work…

baby inoculations!!!....

holding your baby ,too much not enough, i'm pretty sure I could find anything about being a parent to feel guilty about in some way shape or form.

My mum gilt at the moment is in full swing, Alfred is 4months old, I haven't yet left him, not even to pop to the shops.

I know I should but I don't actually want to.

Alfred is breast fed but that comes with guilt too, I love the bond of breastfeeding but feel like I have taken that away from lee.

You would think by my 6th son that I had nailed it but I still feel a lot like I'm winging it.

I haven't broken any of the kids yet so I can't be doing too bad.

Everyone always tries to be the very best mum they can be but we all fail from time to time and some of us fail most of the time.

You can guarantee the times that we will always be in front of a professional for example a social worker or health visitor or in the middle of the playground in front of the headteacher and all of your social peers.

Children have it in for you like that. let's be honest most toddlers are actual arseholes.

My friend Sam's daughter shit on the coffee table in front of the health visitor, The only reason that was quite so funny it's because it wasn't my child.

Joshua's first day of school when I was nervously queuing up with the other parents Joshua said at the top of his big boy voice "mummy does daddy call you bird"…. could've been worse but nonetheless it was embarrassing. I had much worse to come mind you.

Harry had a best friend who was in his words his "brown best friend" and the other boy called Harry his "pink best friend " myself and the other boys mum got called in to speak to the teacher !! This is because they were licking each other to see what they tasted like.

Having to explain to a five-year-old why it's inappropriate to lick another childs face is a bit weird. (keeping a straight face was not easy).

When your child is a toddler and you have family round or go round family is always insist that your toddler gives everybody a hug and kiss goodbye,..... you may wish to remind them that this is no longer appropriate once they start School.

Brody spent a year trying to give his teacher a hug and kiss kiss goodbye at the end of the day, Sweet but again inappropriate.

Ethan kindly bought some unused tampon applicators into school to show his friends the 'rocket launches 'he found, that resulted in an interesting phone call.

I get a phone call from the school at least once a week ,as at least one of the children has injured themselves... nothing serious other than when Ethan broke his nose.

Brody has had several injuries from running into a tree, also a gate.

Why do children let their faces break their fall ??

I always feel bad for the handful of parents that forget it is a non school uniform day. And send the poor little lambs in full uniform.

Or if it is a teacher training day and they send their child to school even though it's not open to pupils , nice try parents.

Or when the your child goes to school without any underwear on!!!

I can always tell when Riley has had PE because he comes out of school with items of clothing on back to front or inside out or shoes on the wrong feet, (he is 10 sort your shit out dude)!!

Make memories with your children they don't stay children forever..
Do Their hand prints. Measure the height on the door frame of their bedrooms.
Make them dance in the rain until they are soaking wet through to their pants.
Let them have ice cream for breakfast on their birthday, and occasionally even when it's not.
Take them to the park in fancy dress you included.
Go on adventures.
By a metal detector.
Run through fountains with your clothes on.
Make up their very own songs with them.
have disco is in the living room.
Wake them up for a sneaky midnight snacks at 8:30pm.
Spin around until you're so dizzy you fall over.
Let them paint your face.
Make cakes.
Blow bubbles.
Mummy always need somebody to lick the spoon.

Have surprises ...have surprises all the time.
Leave gifts on their Pillows.
But notes in their lunchbox.
Take photos every day.
Tickle them till they fart.
Blow raspberries on their tummies.
Read to them.
Let them use a whole bottle of bubble bath in
one go even if it's just once.
Make a den.
Make sock bunnies.
Let them have fun.
let them be silly.
let them be children ....and don't forget to tell
them that you love them every chance you can.

Kids say the funniest things and you find
yourself saying things that you never thought
you would.
Sat in the back of the car with all the children
Brody asked me if I've ever seen a shooting star,
I told them that I had,
he asked me what I wished for ,so I told him
that I wished for a little boy just like Him.
So Riley says "but instead you got Harry"!!!
Even Harry found that funny.

Children ask the most random questions at the
most random times I say random times I mean
when they're supposed to be asleep.

10:45 pm..."mummy how do they make elastic bands???"..." I don't know."..." But mummy you know everything."....." At 10:45 at night mummy knows nothing"!!

Having six boys I must most commonly use the sentences like....put that down, Walk don't run, don't eat that, please get your hand off your penis, stop farting on your brother , no I don't wanna smell that, indoor voices please......

my inner monologue is often saying shut the fuck up and sit down, But that's only because I don't drink and I haven't slept since 2001!!

I've heard myself say random things like stop milking Dora's box! Don't eat eat that snowman's nose.

Who put the kitten in the fridge?

Please stop putting my underwear on your head.

Goldfish don't like hugs.

Please stop talking about poo when I'm eating.

Okay who painted the dog blue?

Mud angels and snow angels are most definitely not the same thing (the school phoned me and got me to bring Ethan a new coat up to the school when he did this).

Why is there a meerkat in your pants?

Don't put in the hamster in your mouth.

One I said today… "I didn't spend a small fortune for this fancy hotel for you to sleep in the cupboard" (something Ethan requested but I didn't let him do) …

I have a few things as a mother I will never apologise for. --
I will not name my child after anybody just because it's a tradition or you, think I should, I do not care if you even like my childs name.
 If you don't like the name of my child, don't pick it for your child , end of discussion.
There is a time and a place for breastfeeding my baby , the time is when my baby is hungry the places where ever I am at that time.... if you don't like it I don't care.
My house will not be immaculate I have far more important mud pies to make then scrubbing my kitchen floors.
I will post pictures of the memories I'm making with my children on my social media if you don't want to see it, unfriend me or just don't look.
I have stretch marks, I have a mummy tummy , I sometimes have hairy legs but it's sometimes also hot outside so I will wear whatever I feel comfortable in.
Yes we are singing badly and loudly on a Sunday morning but that's how we roll.

Children's logic-
My dinner tummy is full up but I have room in my pudding tummy.

If I can't see you then you can't see me.

If bees make honey then wasps make marmite.

Licking my lips is basically the same as washing my face.

Eating toothpaste is basically the same as brushing my teeth.

If I hide Lego in my shoe mummy won't be able to tell that I'm walking differently!

10:45pm is a good time to ask mummy a question.

People must really want to see my bum! (I'm sure every 2 year old boy thinks this because they always want to be naked, no matter where they are)

Monsters must live under my bed even though you couldn't fit a kitten under it.

I know mummy said it would bite me but it probably won't bite me.

I'm sure it won't bite me again.

I will let my face break my fall.

I don't have to adjust my volume I just have to put my hand in front of my mouth and then no one can hear what I'm saying.

I should definitely tell anybody that will listen personal information about my family for example our address, and they definitely need to know about mummies constipation.

I get away with it if I say I did it by accident.

We obviously like to confuse our children….With parent logic-
Mummy is Emie my cousin, know why would you think that she was. Well because Dannie is my auntie. Dannie isn't your real auntie she is just my friend who we call auntie.,,, so is Emie my pretend cousin .. if you wish!!!! Is Kat my pretend auntie… yes… but how come you look like her…, what do you mean I look like her we are ascetically polar opposites.,,, you both have pink in your hair today ,,,.. that is not genetic that is hair dye… oh.,, so what about auntie Kate…., she is a real auntie…. mummy this is confusing… yep.

Don't talk to strangers… go and sit on that mans knee and tell him what you want for Christmas.

Don't eat sweets or your teeth will fall out….. when your teeth fall out the tooth fairy will give you money.

If I take you to the park all day you will definitely go to bed earlier and sleep really well.

I let the children stay up late I'm sure they will lay in ,in the morning.

Use Father Christmas as bribery and the children will be so perfect for all of December.

Counting to 3 makes children stop and listen.

I'm going to spend the first few years of your life teaching you to walk and talk the rest of it telling you to sit down and shut up.

I need to taste test all of your sweets to make sure it's not poisoned. !!!!

Three years ago me and Lee were stood in the kitchen cooking dinner together and Ethan comes in proud as punch and tells us that he has a zombie duck rubber stuck up his nose,
 Ethan says that he put it up there himself he tried to get out but he's just gone further up.
 I take a look and you can only just about see the tip of it right at the top inside his nose.
I give Ethan some tissue to blow his nose but the duck doesn't budge....
 Off to hospital we go.
Ethan is telling anybody that will listen that he has a zombie stuck up his nose.
I had to give what is known as the mothers kiss, this involves blowing in Ethan's mouth, shutting off the clear nostril in the hope that the air will force the obstruction out.
Much to Ethan's delight this just covered my face in his Snot.
After different medical staff trying different sucky things and pickie things we had to go and see the ear nose and throat specIalist.

He was just more willing to use more force than the other doctors were and using a big pair of tweezers held Ethan's head back and yanked out the zombie duck out and we were sent home. Ethan walking back through the hospital holding the small duck above his head shouting to everybody that it was taken back out of his nose.

I took it off him when we got home because he couldn't be trusted not to do it again. 1 year later on the exact same day Ethan fell over at school and hit his face on a bench and broke his nose!!

Harry had the worst habit of attempting to leapfrog over things and not being very good at leapfrogging.!!!!!

Outside the shop he tried to leapfrog over a metal bollard and tore the ligaments in his kneecap.

About five weeks later he tried to leapfrog over a road sign and ripped his trousers. Reveling his spider man pants.

A couple of days after that he tried to leapfrog over a sign outside of the shop and face planted the path.

The best one was when he tried to leap frog a bush and just fell into the bush. "Shouting mummy i'm stuck and I can see an angry bug!!" This boy does not learn.

He is much better at leapfrog now but has taken to learning new stunts on his bike so I am waiting for bike related injuries. (Thankfully he does always wear his helmet)

The funniest injury that I have ever seen a child get is when Brody decided he would become an animal whisperer.
I explained to him that the hamster had not been handled before and he said it wouldn't be a problem.
I told him that the hamster would most definitely bite him.
I admired Brody's bravery as he slowly approached the hamster.
Then I laughed as he recoiled clutching his finger (and made a slight yelp)….the hamster had bit as predicted.
He says it didn't hurt but it did bleed a lot.
Now Ethan wants the hamster to bite him to prove he is as tough as his brother.

Brody tends to do things that completely melts my heart.
 Me and Brody have some great chats on the way home from school.
One day he told me that he had had the most wonderful day as he had a race with the whole class.
He explained how they had to run around the field once.

I asked him why it was particularly good.
He explained that it was amazing because he had come last.
 I asked him to explain why coming last was so amazing.
He said that he was doing quite well, which I believed because he is quite fast.
But he stopped halfway to rescue a snail which I also believe.
And then he said by the time he got to the finish line the whole class was cheering for him and he said it was just wonderful.
His little face was beaming with pride. I gave him a big hug and told him how proud I was of him.
Why do children bring home so many things from school at the end of year it's not like they don't do me pictures at home the rest of the year.
If I was to have kept every single piece of school work that I had ever been given I would need to add an extension to my house to have a special room for it.
I think I did the same as most parents and pick my favourite couple of items each year and file the rest and a B1N!!!
Riley always draws me amazing pictures and he always makes me cards for my birthday or if I've been poorly or if he has missed me when I've been at work for a long time I keep those.

Ethan is always going 100 miles an hour so any drawings he does for me are quite random but they normally make me giggle.

Brody's drawings tend to be of flowers I have a beautiful drawing of a rose that Brody did me recently it makes me smile.

When Harrison was six he had a poem published that was titled "my special mummy" I get tears in my eyes every time I read it .

Joshua painted me a picture of flowers for Mother's Day and wrote on it if mothers were flowers you would be the one I would pick I have that framed in my bedroom.

Alfred's artistic skills are coming along nicely.... and I have copious amounts of foot and hand prints.

I loved doing princess parties, definitely the best job in the world.

I have a snowflake tattoo in Omache. .

Can't be a bad thing to be paid to sing a bit and have loads of kids say they love you.

All the little boys would bring over there little sisters or cousins to meet me, older boys would say they hate me but I'm ok with that.

All the mums would ask for a selfie with me and the dads would ask if I did stag dos!!

I didn't before you wonder.

The most I did in one day was 6parties. It's surprising how much energy it takes out of You. I lost count how many charity events I did and how many times I was in the newspaper As a princess.

It's funny how you take my glasses off , add a wig and a blue dress and people that have known me for years don't recognise me.

Lee got himself a Spider-Man costume, it was one of those spandex all in one type things.

Lee tried it on and we found the as he is not a unic it would be very unacceptable for him to wear that costume around children.

Slightly disappointed that he could not wear it publicly he decided to put it to good use.

Even though only tried to argue his case I told him that he couldn't be a real-life superhero but.... ..

he could convince the children he was the real life Spider-Man.

this was easy because more children are really gullible.

Lee left the Spider-Man costume on the bed, I asked Brody to go and put some clean washing on the end of my bed .

As Brody was walking along the landing Lee shouted out no Brody stop wait...

we heard Brody gasp as he opened the bedroom door...

me and lee both went running into the room and frantically explained that he must not tell anybody the truth.....

 Brody nodded and slowly backed out of the room straight into his bedroom....

 where he promptly told Riley all about the Spider-Man costume on the bed and lee's secret.. a few hrs later Ethan comes running into the living room looks at lee and says "I knew it". ..... 3 years later i'm not overly convinced that the children know that Lee isn't really Spider-Man.

  It's so easy to loose your identity when you become a parent, it's the biggest change in your life.

You forget what it's like to get proper sleep, you always keep an ear open for your baby even when they are 17.

You get used to drinking cold coffee and cutting food one handed.

You can't stand without doing a bop up and down or a side to side rock.

You forgot where all the escalators are in town because you have to use a lift.

You don't care if you have spit, sick or snot on your clothes.

You test the temperature of your own bath with your elbow.

Going to the bathroom is a spectators sport.

You forgot your actual name but turn when anyone calls mum.
You can tell if it's a 'hospital need cry' even from a different room.
You gain super hero powers in the form of magic kisses and eyes in the back of your head.
Silence has never been more terrifying……
so many things will change you forever.
It's not really losing your identity it's just changing it.
I used to be he funny mad one, now I'm the lady with all the boys who is mad.
I think that's why I am so glad that 4,5 and 6 children were boys.
I like being 'the one with all the boys' I honestly wouldn't change it if I could.

My children are actually pretty darn perfect even if I say so myself other than scaring the absolute crap out of me because of how brave they are climbing on things and going near edges, and never putting their hands down when they fall.

I have spent a lot of time with other peoples children through work and having friends with children and I have to say there are no six children I would rather call my own.
Joshua reminds me how old I am and rubbish with technology.

Harrison is the most loved up 14-year-old boy I have ever met his girlfriend is very lucky.
Riley knows everything, I know that because he told me.
Brody has the kindest heart of any nine-year-old child in the world.

Ethan is so incredibly like me when I was his age ,well played Karma.
 I don't know what to say about Alfred as he is a baby,.... He definitely takes after his father , he snores and is obsessed with my boobs but..... he looks at me like I am the only woman in the world.

Chapter 11

Friends and family

I never say that my children are in a broken family ...we are a blended family.
It means the same thing that one sounds nicer than the other.
It's not ideal.... it's not something I picked but it is what it is and I try and make the best out of the situation.
Having more people to love your children can never be a bad thing can it.
When I was growing up I always wanted 2 children, a cottage with white roses growing over the door way, a Labrador. (A husband I presume but I don't remember that actually being part of the dream.)
life doesn't work out the way you dreamed it would when you were 6.

When my brother was born my mum did the great parenting thing of buying me and my sister a doll each so we all had our own babies, great idea,.
my sister got the boy doll and I got the girl doll the only difference being mine had a single locket of hair at the front of his head.

My sister named her boy Thomas , i got a pair of scissors cut the locket off my dolls head and also called it Thomas. I still have my doll.
when I was about 4 I poked the eyes out of my sisters doll and denied all knowledge of it....
this is another example of why I probably should've had some sort of therapy as a child.
That really defines my immediate family, my sister the sensible eldest, my brother the harmless baby and me the devil child.
My mum always did her absolute best by us, juggling being a great mum and a full time teacher.
My dad worked very hard and did the dad things, like putting up flat pack and giving us sweets when mum wasn't looking.
Not a lot as changed.
My sister is still the sensible/normal one with a husband and 3 children.
My brother is over 6ft but still the baby, he can do stupid stuff but he gets away with it.
He has a wife and 2 children. T

hen you have me still the devil child, I fuck up, I fuck up a lot…. But I try to be a good person and the best mum my boys could wish for.

Me and my brother spent many years being best of friends, I was a bit of a tomboy so enjoyed making mud pies with James over playing dollies with Kate.

Me and James always had a very immature friendship.

Do you remember that game where you make the okay sign with your hand and hold it lower than your waist and if the other person looks at it you get to punch them in the arm….

Me and Jamie started playing that game when we were about 14 and continue playing it until we were maybe 22. …

It's amazing how extreme the game can get. Me and James were playing the game in a posh restaurant we were at for my mum's 50th birthday , dad made us move seats so we couldn't play anymore .

Just had got the last punch in, so the next day I took a photo of my hand doing the ok signh, I printed it off.

Walked 2miles to my brothers house , posted the photo through his door, waited till I saw him pick it up and look at it,…. I open the door punched him in the arm and ran away.

WINNER!!!

One year for my birthday my brother farted into an empty drink bottle and gave it to me two weeks later. .....
I'm not exaggerating when I say I have smelt better dead people.
The best birthday gift James ever gave me was the greatest gift of all, the gift of a child's laughter .... Sort of... James text me saying "happy birthday , I have got you the greatest gift in the world!!!" So I called him and asked what this gift was.... He replied "the gift of a child's laughter " he then did a really creepy giggle and then hung up!!!

My apple grandparents are still alive and kicking, grandad does most of the kicking.
I have a great relationship with my grandad.
I wind him up but I think it keeps him young.
I have never heard my grandad swear and I have only ever seen him really angry twice.
Once was the first time he saw me after my mum informed him that I was pregnant at the age of 17 , He said "frankly Elizabeth I don't know whether to give you a hug or smack your bottom "
I know he was angry and I don't blame him it definitely came from a place of love.

Another time was when the builders next door to my house where checking debris in my garden and the children wanted to play in the garden so my grandad really gave him what for.,,,
I have never seen him wave that arthritic finger with such gumption.
Grandad used to run the Suffolk county council as the chief executive (I think that's right)
The children like to google him and find pictures of him with the Queen.
I'm convinced that granny Apple was born a sweet old lady (I obviously didn't know her when she was little that would just be weird and impossible) but the whole of my life certainly she has just been the most incredible sweet , kind old lady. She is little and adorable like a puppy, just just want to cuddle her.

My dad parents are a long time passed, granny died of motor neurones disease 15 years ago.
 Grandad died 10 years after her.
Both completely fascinating and amazing people.
I was pregnant with Harrison when granny died and at her funeral I absolutely lost my shit, like you see on eastenders.
That was the first moment I realise just how cruel life could be.
And I went through all of the stages of grief but was stuck on angry for a really long time.

I still get upset, i miss her very much when I think about her. I
f I was to have had a daughter or if I ever have a daughter I would like her name as my daughter's middle name.
My grandad was a total gentleman in every sense of the word, The world would be a better place with more people like my grandparents that's for sure.

My dad has one sister, my mum has two sisters and I have three cousins ,all girls.
We are a close family where it counts you know for things like birthdays ,Christmases , weddings and funerals. Stuff like that.
My two adult cousins are ridiculously intelligent and I am incredibly jealous of them, waiting for them to hurry up and have babies for me to play with.
My blood family is relatively small when I think about it, me and my children make up the vast proportion of the family.
I don't see my extended family every day or even every month but they only know where I am if they need me.

I have a massive chosen family , I have my LGBTQ+ family, my work family, my mummy friends family, lots of other people's children I consider family.

Lee always says blood makes you a relative and loyalty makes you family.

As you get older you realise that it's ok if your parents don't like you the same as they like your siblings....

My dad is hardly going to have a pint and watch the football with me (mainly coz I hate beer and football) me and mum are both fabulous but very different people.

That's just fine.

I will admit I felt a bit left out when I was younger but I didn't help myself by being a devil child.

My behavior has been somewhat challenging throughout most of my life. That made me the black sheep and I still am in a lot of ways.

My friends/chosen family.... You are a lucky bunch.

I would do anything for anyone (within reason) and I go the extra mile for my friends.

Don't ask me to lie for you though, not that I'm overly moral it's more the fact that I can't lie without involving pterodactyls ,or other things that make it really obvious that I'm talking utter shit.

I once ate the last biscuit that was being saved for lee and I told him a mummy pterodactyl flew in the window and stole it to feed her baby, I went into great detail about the trees outside the front of our house being perfect the habitat for pterodactyls!!!

Unfortunately this goes for secrets too, I can only keep a secret if no one asks be about it.
If nobody questions me about the said secret then I will take it to the grave with me ,other than lee tell him everything.
 I can't even keep nice secrets from lee, he has never opened a Christmas gift from me on Christmas Day because I give it to him as soon as I get it,...the act of hiding something from him feels like I am hiding something from him and not in a good way.
 I do buy the best gifts, really thoughtful.
What they lack in monetary value they make up for it in sentimental.
I have made many friends cry with my gifts.
I am horrible to buy for, the worst thing is I won't want to hurt your feelings but my face will tell you I hate it at the same time my mouth says something else.
I use lines like… wow I haven't seen one of them before and …. Wow look at all the colours!!!
 I would rather you got your kids to make me a card or we just go out for dinner than you attempt to buy me a jumper or an ornament.

I have single-handedly thrown 8 baby showers, 4 hen nights and 3 surprise birthday parties I even have organised a whole wedding (That wasn't mine) .
I am good at organising stuff, I make up my own games and make my own cupcakes.
I used to run ladies nights in the night club' Pals'. They involved a massive Ann summers party, a stripper and drinking games. I was everyone's "best bud" when I held auditions for strippers!!!

A great gift that any friend would appreciate is a signed framed photo of yourself doing a double thumbs up. I don't know anyone that wouldn't want that. I know I would appreciate it if you gave me that as a gift. (i'm only half joking).
I was popular at school , I had almost too many friends.
Not enough days in the week or hrs in the day for everyone but we had so much fun.
 House parties , karaoke at the pub and the occasional homework/study group.
I still see a few of my friends from school but on the most part life got in the way and we lost contact other than through social media.

My best girlfriend who has been there with me through thick and thin for the last 12 years is Kat.

You absolutely do my head in at times but I wouldn't change you for the world.

Amount of times I have walked into your house and made myself at home.

The time where I walked in and you told me that you were in bed naked so I took off my close walking up the stairs and got in with you!

I made sure I was round the day you had your new sofas delivered so I could pick which one was going to be mine.

The time you had me kicked out of pound land (yes it was your fault).

The many times you had to be my handler when I was dressed as Elsa (As Disney princesses don't wear glasses I was virtually Blind).

The time where we both had to get changed in the back of the Taxi.

I have made you do to charity 5K runs with me and I know you despise running ,you begrudge even running a bath.

You even let me in your car covered in mud after the mud run.

You have put up with my premenstrual hungry days (It's a good job you live opposite a shop).

We have laughed together over so many things, my favourite has to be the lady at mums N tots.

It is definitely unnecessary to have both breasts out when you are feeding one single baby.

The look on her face still makes me smile when you asked her if she was airing the other boob or waiting for another baby to arrive.

We have had so many lunches together I could definitely order for you if I had to.

The best thing you have ever done for me is bring my placenta home from the hospital fand keep it in your freezer for a month till I was ready to bury it in with a rose bush.

When you came to the hospital only minutes after I had given birth and you stood next to the hospital bed asking what it is your standing in ha ha ha fuck knows but it definitely contains my DNA.

The fact she kept sending me pictures of food she was cooking saying it could do with some of my placenta in I,t was both unnecessary and disgusting but expect from you.

There are two things that I am going to do with you that we haven't done before ....one is get drunk with you because we have never actually done that and two we will set up a business together I don't know what doing but it needs to be done.

Having lots of children you meet lots of your children's friends parents and occasionally you make friends with them.

Admittedly nine times out of 10 I would rather have the kids round to make cupcakes then I would have to do adult stuff with the adults.

But I have made a few great friends this way.
Dannie you are a star and I love you just as
much as I love your 3 beautiful daughters.
 Sarah you do the most amazing job and I love
that you give me a hug every day.
Rubina , Clair, Vicky. Jenna, you got this
mummas and I love you all... The rest of you
lovely lot have asked that I don't talk about you
in my book but know that you rock and I love
you.
James you are a rubbish gay but a great friend ,
you have my back and it means a lot but I'm
going to have to tell the story about your cock.
 Many years ago I used to breed my Chihuahua
called Woody.
James knew this about me.
So when he decided to give breeding dogs a go
with his beautiful dog Elliot , Who better than to
ask advice than me .
.... James decided he would use a well-known
pet site to advertise Elliot up for stud.
me and James stod behind the bar in the arb set
to work with Elliott's stud page.
James didn't have a clue so I basically did
everything on his phone for him.
It got to the part where you had to upload the
photos of your dog.
So without thinking I pressed on the button to
select image from James's photo library on his
phone.

If anyone has ever done this you will know that it comes up with your most recent photos you have taken first.

It turns out that James had been on grinder before our shift in the pub, and had taken a 'selfie 'in the bath full mast!!!

In the shock of seeing James 's hard cock I squealed and chucked James phone back at him.

It took a good two hours for us to stop being red cheeked and giggling at each other.

At this point we decided we had better finish the add but I would let James upload the Photo of the dog.

And it was then that he found out that in my haste I had pressed upload and James had been up for stud for the last two hrs.

Sorry not sorry…, funny as fuck.

I made some really great friends at work, it takes a special kind of person to be a support worker I honestly believe that.

So if nothing else we have that in common .

I particularly clicked with Zeena , Corin, Heather and Tom.

Working long shifts with you guys made it barely seem like work at all.

Corin was the best to work with because he was amazing at the paperwork and I was great at the other bits.

I love making new work friends but you won't catch me at the Christmas party, sorry but any free time I have over Christmas I will be with my family not anything that reminds me of work,
 but I will get you a secret Santa gift (it will be a copy of my book so not very secret).

It sounds completely cliche but my all-time best friend, my partner in crime, my Sole mate is my whale Lee.

Finding couple friends is really hard, either I don't like one of them or Lee doesn't like one of them.
or they have really annoying children.
I will make a friend with somebody at work be introduced to their partner and the first thing I'm thinking is ….will lee you get on with them.
 Lee is very intolerant of people with a low IQ. More than once we have gone out for dinner with a couple friends and Lee has said that it's absolutely not going to work out.
 He is happy for me to be friends with whoever I want to be friends with but if somebody doesn't know the difference between pastrami and bacon , because they don't like pork!!!!!
 Lee is not going to tolerate this kind of behaviour!!!!

I don't think this person is going to want to be friends with me after reading this book because I've never had this conversation with them but they would exactly who I'm talking about .

Lee just said whilst reading this over my shoulder that she stupid and wouldn't know I was talking about her .
I say lee is the reason we don't have couple friends.
I do love having a dinner party and we normally have Lee's brother Paul and his partner Sonia round for dinner parties.
I like cooking and socialising Lee likes eating the food that I have cooked.
Lee is also happy that it pleases his mum to be friends with his brother.
Even if he does call his brother sloppy bollocks and that pisses him off.
I have Sonia stored in my phone as big sis.
I'm fully aware that I do have a big sister but I get on as a friend more with Sonia so we are more like sisters or at least the sort of sisters that you want to be, you know like you see on the telly s....isters brushing each other's hair and stuff.
Lee is a typical big brother to Paul, Lee is horrible to him and Paul puts up with it.

Lee's mum only lives down the road and I love going to see her,

Lee makes up stuff to try and get me in trouble with her.

He tells her that I don't hold his hand when crossing the road,

he tells her that he cooked for Paul and Sonia the other day, and I spat in the food and a multitude of other lies which makes Sue look at me and shake her head.

But she knows he's joking and she loves me of course.

Every time I suggest going to visit Mum Lee makes up some stupid excuses ,like we've already seen her this year.

He is sort of right that we don't have enough time to see her because the "popping in for a quick visit "always ends up being a whole day. We can never forget mum's birthday because it is the same day as Christmas but as I remind lee that this is not an excuse to only buy her one gift. Lee's reasoning is that he doesn't even buy Jesus a gift so why would his mum get 2!!

Unfortunately lee's father Tony passed away 22 years ago , I'm not going to talk about that but I know that he would've been incredibly proud of his sons and grandchildren.

I wish I got to meet him.

What do you think that all of my friends have in common???

It is that they understand that you don't need to put out somebody elses flame to make yours brighter.
Let your friends shine and if the light starts to fade make sure you're the one adding fuel.
Nobody likes somebody that pisses on anyone's parade.
You never truly lose a friend you just sometimes find out who the real ones are. .....

Chapter 12

Bucket list

I've never really actually sat down and written a bucket List.
Had I have done a bucket list 20 years ago I'm sure I would've coincidentally of ticked some things off it by now.

Whenever people have spoken about things they've done from their bucket list I've always thought that , that doesn't really sound like something that would even be on my list.

I sit there smiling and nodding as my friend Zayn is talking about backpacking for 6 months and gathering droppings from a Tibetan mountain goat, and I can't help but think I really don't give a shit.

Maybe I should give a shit but I don't I just don't give a shit.

It's so great if you have done something that you've always wanted to do but I don't understand why you would want to go backpacking when they're perfectly nice hotels and things.

I once stayed in a tent in my own back garden and ordered pizza.

A caravan is the most Bear Grylls I will go.

Unless it was for charity ,or maybe a game show where I could win a large amount of money, I just don't get it.

I would definitely get dirty hands if I went backpacking and we know I don't like dirty hands.

Me and Lee go for very long walks we have walked up to 25 miles in a day.

But I didn't have to shit in a hole or drink my own piss.

And since when is all of this risk behaviour things that people want to put on their bucket list.

No I don't want to go free diving with sharks what are you mad.

Even with one of those cages I'm not that interested.

We all know with my luck I would come on my period the exact moment I was plunged into the water and it would attract one of those clever sharks that was able to get into the cage.

And I probably wouldn't get killed I would just lose my favourite hand or a boob.

Yep that's what would happen I would have one boob bitten off.

And it wouldn't leave enough of my flesh for reconstructive surgery ,so I would have to decide whether they should just leave me with one or take both off.

I would probably ask them to just leave the one it would be more of a talking piece.

I don't wanna jump out of things or off things, I have seen other peoples videos and you don't look attractive with your cheeks flapping around the place in the wind.

I'm not good under pressure or following instructions. …..Ask my dad what happened when he asked me to pull the rope when we were on his Boat…..

i'm not saying it was anyone's fault but my hair got wet.

Publishing a book...... that's going on the bucket list hopefully along with a big tick next to it very soon.

I would like to own a chow-chow in my lifetime. One of the ones that look like a panda.
Or one that is willing to let me die it's hair to look like a panda.
 Or if you could genetically modify a real panda so it would make for a good pet that would be good .
 Panders just go with everything.
How are you going to accessorise that little black dress I hear you ask , well I will just bring my panda.
Panda Pete is a good name for a panda.
Not too sure but I think I will call my chowchow...... panda.

I would like to go to Italy with Lee for the food and the artwork.
90% the food and maybe 10%the art thingy but we tell people it's 50/50 so we sound less like fat pigs.

I would love to do a walk or climb for charity. Kilimanjaro for MND would be ideal.

Would have to wait till the kids were much older because I wouldn't leave the country without thematic this age.
Or maybe a small walk that I could do in a day…. I would have to raise a lot before you would get me in a tent.

Most people want to see sights of the world like the Grand Canyon or the Great Wall of China but I have no desire to do that sort of thing.. maybe I'm just not that cultured.
I am content having seen them in books and on the Tv.

I'm desperate to see the Northern Lights but as a photographer more than the trip.
I want to get "the photo" with the pinks and blues and have it printed on a massive canvas and put on the ceiling above (I would have to take the mirror down first… eew….joking) .

I have always wanted to live in a house big enough to have a baby grand piano under the staircase and a bath with gold feet.
I have no problem working really hard to get there.

After I am done with it I would like to donate my womb.
I always call it my second heart as it gave my children life.

I couldn't imagine not being able to have children so be be able to give someone my second heart so they could create life would surly be the best gift ever.

 Not sure if it's possible to be done whilst I'm still alive but I hope it is, if not I just hope that it's donated once I'm dead.

I want to hold a monkey, but only if it can be done in a totally animal cruelty Free way.
I have jokes for years about wanting a chimp called Dave, I would get him to ride a mobility scooter ,smoke cigars wear a fez and a tutu and stick his middle finger up at people.
unfortunately this definitely couldn't be done without involving some kind of animal cruelty which I am against so it will just have to be a comical mental image.

I would like long hair, not extensions or a wig but my own real long hair.
So long that it would cover all the rude bits if I was naked.
 Like a mermaid. My hair grows so slowly that I would have to live till I was 207 to be able to tick this one off but I will give it a go.

I would like to give talks in schools about living with dyslexia.

I want to be an adult bridesmaid. I have only
ever been a child bridesmaid .
I would be a great bridesmaid.
I'm good at walking down the isle.
 I will were pretty much anything you ask me to
and I will definitely make you look good.

I am at about 5k already but I want to raise 10k
for CRUK. On my just giving page
I am 100% sure I will do it.

Go to university and finally my degree.
I don't know what in but I know I want one.
That would go in a frame right at the top of all
the others in the loo.

Taking the kids to Disneyland has to be on my
bucket list I'm not too sure any of them are that
bothered about going but I thought it was
magical when I went and I would love to share
that with the boys.

Chapter 13

Bits and bobs

Some things about me you still don't know after reading this book but you will know after reading this bit-
I have a stone stuck in my forehead that has been there since I was 2,
you can see it ,you can feel it and it's kind of disgusting.

I have a heart shaped uterus which sounds really cute but if you google images you will see that it is not.

I have never seen the Sound of Music.

I don't instantly know the time on a 24-hour clock I have to work it out.

My favourite body part is my thumbs because they remind me of a funny little fat men.
My hair is naturally curly and I don't know what my natural hair colour is anymore.

I'm a sucker for an ugly animal if you show me a photo of a dog with one eye, no teeth, a missing leg and it only walks backwards I am going to want it .
Hence Nancy.

 Like a baby I don't sleep through the night. I don't wake up because I need anything.
It's just to double check where I am and that all is in good order.

 I like things perpendicular. If it's not a right angle it's a wrong angle.

Me and lee have been paranormal investigators for collectively around 20 years. (Read BAPRI spirit files)

I collect Herman bears and I talk to them just in case 'toy story' is real

Baby names I like (it's good to have a stand by list ready for baby 7 if we ever decide to be that crazy)

Boys names –

George
Sidney
Frankie
Erick
Rex
Loxley
Spencer

Girls names-

Bluebell
Elise
Dorothy
Ellen
Violet
lacy

I really like trees, all trees are great. We can't live without trees.

I like willow trees the best.

My stretch marks remind me of a Silver birch tree.

I like taking photos of the boys with trees as it adds great texture.

I like banana flavored things ,like those little foam banana sweets and banana milkshake and anything banana flavored but I'm not very keen on actual bananas.

I love strawberries but I hate anything strawberry flavored.

And I love watermelon everything including actual watermelons.

I don't eat eggs or processed ham, I often tell people this is for ethical reasons but it's actually just because I don't like anything that tastes the same as farts smell.

I'm scared of the dentists only because I don't like people touching my face no other reason.

If you ever make too much buttercream just add some flour and an egg and you have yourself a tasty cookie mix.

I don't think it's normal if you're not at least a little bit scared of the dark.

My favourite meal is probably spaghetti Bolognese but only if I cook it.
I don't like anybody else's spaghetti Bolognese not even in a nice restaurants.

My mum is a pretty good cook but cannot make custard for love nor money.

I have a pretty decent imagination but this is to the detriment of my sleep , because often the stuff that I think about ……..for example what I would do if I won the lottery I find that way more entertaining than actually sleeping so I spend six hours with my thoughts rather than catching some important sleep.

I don't believe you can have odds socks, you have just created two new pairs!

Even though I can tie shoelaces up I never tire the shoelaces up on my trainers I just tuck the laces in.

I take great pleasure in trying to wind up medical staff but find that they often have no sense of humor.

When the nurse asked me to take my clothes off from the waist down ready for my smear test I asked her if she was going to buy me dinner first.

When I had my six week check after giving birth I asked the doctor if I could drive he said yes , I asked him if I could play the piano he said of course ,why wouldn't you be able to.

then I told him that I could do neither before having a baby.....again he did not find this funny. When they ask what you are allergic to, I first of all tell them plasters because that's quite important when you are in hospital,

Then I go on to tell them of all the different beauty products that I am allergic to , definitely less important.

I can't whistle, nor do I have any want or need to.

If I could pick anybody to have dinner with dead or alive, I would pick Michael Jackson. (dont know why, I just would like to meet him)

I changed my middle name from Rebecca to Rose because I preferred it, it is also sort of my mum's name and I could!

I've had my TV for almost 4 years and I still don't know how to work it.

What do you do if you are riding a giraffe and being chased by a lion and a rhino?? Get your drunk arse of the carousel!!

There are many reasons that me and Lee don't drink alcohol anymore, it started four years ago when we decided to do a dry year for charity and we just don't really see the point in drinking again.
It's expensive, it makes the room spin, (if you put your foot on the floor when laying in bed it does work to stop the spinning) there are other drinks I like the taste of and it makes you irresponsible if you are drunk around children and we are always around children.
I'm not saying we will never touch a drop of alcohol again I'm just saying that we don't have it in the house and if you offer me a drink it will more likely to be coffee or water I will ask for.

When people ask men if they dress to the left or the right I know what that means ,but I don't understand the answer.
if they say they dress to the right for example does that mean they have put their bits to the right hand side or the left hand side.

I presume it means what side is your penis but if you're taking your inner legs seem they take it from the other side so that would mean that the side your clothes are cut to so are you dressed to that side???
 And I have just really confuse myself so if you know what the hell I'm going on about you are clearly a genius.

My favourite colour is pink but specifically a dusky pink I don't like bubblegum pink ,baby pink neon pink, hot pink just dusky pink.

"Reach for the moon even if you miss you will land among the stars."This is one of my favourite sayings because it's true.
I would always rather regret doing something that I have done, than live the rest of my life regretting not doing it at all.

I never realised how vulnerable it makes feel writing about yourself and even though I'm mostly just joking I still feel pretty naked.

I have twice won a competition for having the most random thing in my handbag.
 Both of these competitions were held at make up buying parties I can't even remember the brand.

The first time my one with a tooth (One of the children had lost a tooth that week and it was in the bottom of my handbag).
The second time was a Lego fish that Joshua had made for me.
Right now I think the most random thing I have in my handbag is a dead crab in resin keyring that I won in a penny machine yesterday!

I didn't write this book in any particular order just sort of when things came to mind or my memory was provoked by something.
I have realised I could've filled at least three books of exactly the same nature.
Maybe I will knock them out one day.
 I will see how this one is received.

I promise that I will sign any books passed to me, but I will only sign them with my name because I can guarantee I know how to spell that your name might be a bit trickier for me.

Love and unicorns.....

(this book is a bit wonky and I should of paid for a proper edit... but I didn't)